PRAYERS FOR PRISONERS

EDWARD DEWEESE

PRAYERS FOR PRISONERS

Art Direction: Michele Wetherbee
Cover design & illustration: Stefan Gutermuth
Interior design, typesetting, and layout: Nancy Cole

Library of Congress Cataloging-in-Publication Data

DeWeese, Edward, 1930-
Prayers for prisoners / Edward DeWeese. — [Rev. ed.]
p. cm.
ISBN 0-8358-0789-4 (pbk.)
1. Prisoners—Prayer-books and devotions—English. 2. Devotional calendars. I. Title.
BV4595.D48 1997
242'.68—dc20 96-28985
CIP

ISBN 0-8358-0789-4
Printed in the United States of America
First printing: March 1997 (5)

Previously published in a slightly different version by J. Countryman Publishers, Houston, Texas. © 1989 by C & D International.

Contents

FOREWORD

Ed DeWeese is a brother who knows what it is to be locked behind bars. He knows the loneliness, pain, and despair that inmates face; yet he also knows the amazing grace of our Lord and what it is to be set free in Jesus Christ. And he knows the peace and personal growth that come only through a diligent, serious study of the scriptures.

I am delighted that Ed has put together this book of devotions. Each day's material presents a nugget of scripture, prayer, and reflection designed specifically for those in prison. Ed's experiences and insights offer a guide through the basics of Christian discipleship.

If you are in prison, I urge you to pursue these devotions faithfully each day. Root yourself in the word of God, in constant communication with God, and in fellowship with others who know God. If you do so, God will draw you ever closer; and you will learn the most precious truth of life—what Paul once wrote from a prison cell: "I have the strength to face all conditions by the power that Christ gives me" (Phil. 4:13).

— CHARLES W. COLSON
Chairman and Founder of Prison Fellowship

✷

This book of devotions was written to help persons discover God's presence while they are in prison. The author, Ed DeWeese, writes out of his own experience and discovery. His daily devotions seek to deal with the many feelings and frustrations experienced by one who is suddenly separated from family, friends, and society by means of imprisonment.

Ed demonstrates a remarkable sensitivity to the prisoner's special needs that can only be understood by one who has been there. When our lives are overwhelmed with rapid, unbelievable change, when we feel forsaken, alone, and deeply hurt, we have a desperate need to discover the presence of God. If we can find God, if we can know that God is present, *we can make it*.

I believe the devotions in *Prayers for Prisoners* can enable us to see God at work in all the events around us, in our world, and even in the shattering experience of imprisonment. I believe these devotions can lead one to faith in God. When faith opens our eyes and ears, we can sense the possibilities God has for us. My prayer is that many will find here a path on which the first steps of their *new life* will be taken.

— ROBERT C. MORGAN
Resident Bishop
The Louisville Episcopal Area; The United Methodist Church

✷

One only has to page through the Bible or even a good history of the lives of holy men and women over the years to see how many of them were in jail. Old Testament prophets, Jesus himself, the Apostle Paul, many early Christians, and many in our own lifetime are in prison now or have been in prison.

As a fellow Christian Ed DeWeese is one who has walked in the footsteps of all those who have spent time in prison. In his own life he has turned that time of pain and suffering into a time of grace. Through this book he offers insights to others in hope that they too might use this time to grow in faith.

I am happy to be able to recommend *Prayers for Prisoners* to all who are in prison ministry or who are inmates. My prayer is that through these pages and the grace of the Lord you will be able to use the insights in these pages to make giant steps in your spiritual journey. Along with the "good thief," may you share paradise with your Lord some day. I think that you will find the reflections of this book good tools toward that end.

— THE REVEREND GEORGE E. GOODBOUT
Director of Pastoral Care
Our Lady of the Lakes Regional Medical Center, Baton Rouge, LA
and Director of Pastoral Care
Our Lady of the Lakes Regional Medical Center, Lafayette, LA

How to Use This Book

This book of devotions for prisoners came out of Ed DeWeese's experiences in the state penitentiary at Parchman, Mississippi, and in the Mississippi Restitution–Correctional Center at Pascagoula, Mississippi. At Parchman Ed DeWeese organized Bible study groups in his camp, Unit 29, and in the R and D Center (Receiving and Diagnostic Center). The groups needed materials with which to work. As individuals they also needed devotional guides written specifically for prisoners.

As you use this book, you may use it as your personal devotional guide. Use one page each day, reading and thinking about the Bible verses. Then use the prayer as a guide. Be led of the Lord, however, to pray your own prayer as you feel the need. Then let the Thought for the Day be a seed in your mind for that day.

You may use this book for group devotions in your camp. Gather some inmates together. Read the page for that day. Discuss the Bible verses, and talk about the Thought for the Day. Invite each group member who wishes to pray, to do so.

Use this book for a nineteen-week period. Keep a chart for each day that you read your page and have your prayer, so you can watch yourself grow in the spirit of the Lord.

Use this book with your families. At home they can read and study the same page that you read and study each day. This practice will allow you to have family prayer even though you are away from home.

Special Word to Prison Chaplains: Distribute copies of *Prayers for Prisoners* among the prisoners. It will help them draw close to the Lord and find the strength they need day by day.

Crisis Scripture Guide

Alcohol and Substance Abuse—Proverbs 20:1; Daniel 1:8; 1 Corinthians 6:19-20
Anger—Proverbs 14:29; Ecclesiastes 7:9; Ephesians 4:26; Ephesians 4:31-32
Children—Proverbs 22:6; Matthew 19:13-14; Ephesians 6:4
Confusion—Isaiah 50:7; 1 Corinthians 14:33; James 3:16-18
Danger—Psalm 46:1; Psalm 91; Psalm 121:5-8; 2 Timothy 4:16-18
Death—Isaiah 25:8; Romans 14:8; Revelation 21:4
Decision-making—Deuteronomy 30:19; Psalm 25:12; Proverbs 3:5-6
Depression—Psalm 38:4-9; Philippians 4:8; 1 Thessalonians 5:16-18
Despair—Psalm 27:14; 2 Corinthians 4:8-9; Galatians 6:9
Discouragement—Psalm 31:24; Psalm 138:7-8; Hebrews 10:35-36
Divorce—Matthew 5:31-32; Mark 10:2-12; Luke 16:18
Exhaustion—Psalm 55:22; Isaiah 40:29-31; Matthew 11:28-30
Failure—Romans 8:28; 2 Corinthians 4:8-9; 1 Timothy 6:10-11
Fear—Isaiah 41:10; John 14:27; 1 John 4:18
Financial Trouble—Matthew 6:31-33; 2 Corinthians 9:6-8; Philippians 4:19
Grief—Psalm 23; 2 Corinthians 1:3-4; Revelation 21:4
Illness—Proverbs 4:20-22; James 5:14-15; 3 John 2
Isolation—Romans 8:35-39; Philippians 4:4; Revelation 3:20
Loneliness—1 Samuel 12:22; John 14:1-3; John 14:18
Lust—Galatians 5:16-17; 2 Timothy 2:22; James 1:13-15
Marriage—Genesis 2:18, 24; Proverbs 18:22; Hebrews 13:4
Old Age—Psalm 73:26; Psalm 90:12; Titus 2:2-4
Rebellion—Isaiah 1:19-20; Romans 6:12-13; 1 Peter 5:5-6
Rejection—Deuteronomy 31:6; Psalm 27:10; Psalm 147:3
Salvation—John 3:16; Romans 6:23; Romans 10:9-10, 13
Stress— Psalm 107:5-7; Isaiah 30:18; Matthew 11:28-30

Suffering—Psalm 25:16-18; John 9:1-3; 1 Peter 2:20-21
Temptation—1 Corinthians 10:12-13; Hebrews 2:18; James 1:12-13
Trials—Psalm 34:17-19; Psalm 56:11-13; 1 Peter 4:12-13
Uncertainty—Psalm 23; Psalm 37:4-5; Isaiah 28:16
Weakness—Isaiah 40:31; 2 Corinthians 12:8-10; Philippians 4:13
Worry—Matthew 6:25-34; John 14:27; Philippians 4:5-8

INTRODUCTION

Jesus Christ loves you! You may be in a city or county jail. You may be hungry or lonely. You may feel afraid, resentful, ashamed. *Jesus Christ loves you!*

Your jail may be dirty and dark, cold or hot. Roaches may crawl the walls and the food may be awful. *Jesus Christ loves you!*

You may be in a state penitentiary. You may be in a noisy, crowded, confined cellblock. You may be craving a good meal, fresh air, a quiet place to think and rest. *Jesus Christ loves you!*

You may be in solitary, alone in a tight little cell. You may be a lifer. You may be on death row. *Jesus Christ loves you!*

You may be in a federal pen. You may have been stripped of the prestige and power of an office and found yourself in a federal pen, without your former dignity and respect. You may hear officers barking orders instead of you telling others what to do. You may feel crushed, hopeless, at the end of your rope. You may feel your world has come to an end. It has not!

Whoever you are, wherever you are in the world, *Jesus Christ loves you!* For you were *made in God's image!* "Then God said, 'And now we will make human beings; they will be like us and resemble us' " (Gen. 1:26).

Jesus Christ loves you! Christ died for you! "For God loved the world so much that he gave his only Son, so that everyone who believes in him may not die but have eternal life" (John 3:16). Jesus Christ is the Son of God, the Savior of the world—*and your Savior too!*

The first sermon Jesus preached was about *being in prison*. That proves how important you are to God. What did Jesus say?

> The Spirit of the Lord is upon me,
> because he has chosen me to bring good news
> to the poor.

> He has sent me to proclaim liberty to the captives
> and recovery of sight to the blind,
> to set free the oppressed.
>
> — Luke 4:18

Jesus longed for people to be free—*not to be in prison!* He wants you to be free. He wants you to live in God's will. If you had been living by *God's will,* you would not have been sent to prison. You would not have done the thing that sent you here.

But now that you are in prison, if you live by God's will while you are here, you will be free sooner than if you do not live by God's will.

Jesus Christ, the Son of God, was a prisoner too. He was accused, arrested, tried, convicted, sentenced, and executed. Jesus was accused by the Pharisees of disturbing the peace. He was accused of wanting to replace the king.

The Romans arrested Jesus. The high priest tried him. The governor also tried him. He was sentenced to death. He was executed on a cross. He knows what you are going through!

Did your friends leave you? Did people insult you? Did they make cruel jokes about you? Did they take your clothes? Did they force strange clothes on you? Did they hit you? They did all these things to Jesus!

Friday was the day of his execution. After Friday came Sunday. Sunday was the day of his rising from the dead. After Jesus was the executed criminal, he was the risen Savior!

After your Friday—your days in prison—will come your Sunday—your day of joy and freedom! The *extra good news* is that even while you are behind those locked gates, you can have your Sunday of joy and victory through Jesus Christ.

"Some, however, did receive him and believed in him; so he gave them the right to become God's children" (John 1:12).

Praise the Lord! You can have the power of God to

become a son or daughter of God right where you are. You can have the power of God. Thank you, Lord!

This book offers you some Bible verses, some prayers, and some thoughts to help you live—even in prison—as a son or daughter of God. They will help you *live in* the Lord! And God will help you solve your problems, will open doors for you, and will heal your heartaches.

> Joseph's master was furious and had Joseph arrested and put in the prison where the king's prisoners were kept, and there he stayed. But the LORD was with Joseph and blessed him so that the jailer was pleased with him.
>
> — Genesis 39:19-21

WEEK ONE: TO KNOW MYSELF

Day 1 ✵ I Was Made by God

BIBLE VERSE: Acknowledge that the LORD is God.
He made us, and we belong to him;
we are his people, we are his flock.
— Psalm 100:3

PRAYER: O Lord, I have often asked myself, *Where did I come from?* Sometimes I feel I was an accident, just a result of two people having sex. Sometimes I feel I wasn't wanted.

But, God, I know I have to be more than that. Now I read in your word that you made me. That means I am special to you. That means you care about me. That lets me know where I came from. You made me! Thank you, Lord! In Jesus' name. Amen.

THOUGHT FOR THE DAY: In the book *The Fire Next Time,* James Baldwin writes, "Know whence you came. If you know whence you came, there is really no limit to where you can go."[1]

You came from God. You were made by God. You were no accident of sex. You were created by God for companionship with God! Knowing that, there is no limit to what you can become in Christ.

---

[1]James Baldwin, *The Fire Next Time* (New York: Dell Publishing Co., 1962), pp. 18-19.

WEEK ONE: TO KNOW MYSELF

Day 2 ✷ I Was Made in God's Image

BIBLE VERSE: So God created human beings, making them to be like himself. He created them male and female.

— Genesis 1:27

PRAYER: God, you made the whole world. And then you made people. Your word says that you made us in your image, to be like you.

This means I was made in your image—I was made to be like you. I don't feel as though I was made like you. But you said that I was. I must be made for something better than I have been living, God. I haven't been living like you. I know that.

God, help me know that I was made in your image. Help me think and act more like I was made like you. In Jesus' name I pray. Amen.

THOUGHT FOR THE DAY: You have a mirror. When you look into your mirror, you see yourself. You see your eyes, your nose, your mouth—as they are. Yet the mirror is not you. It shows your image. You are an image of God, made in God's likeness.

WEEK ONE: TO KNOW MYSELF

Day 3 ✷ I Am a Child of God

BIBLE VERSE: God's Spirit joins himself to our spirits to declare that we are God's children. Since we are his children, we will possess the blessings he keeps for his people, and we will also possess with Christ what God has kept for him; for if we share Christ's suffering, we will also share his glory.

— Romans 8:16-17

PRAYER: God, I seek to be led by your Spirit while I am here in prison. I crave to be your child. I hunger to know you as my Parent. I rejoice, O God, that even here in prison you claim me as your child and need me to give witness to you. I am your child—your son, daughter—in Christ! Praise your name, O Lord, forever and ever! In Jesus' name. Amen.

THOUGHT FOR THE DAY: A few days ago my daughter came to see me. She is a grown young lady now. She looked so pretty. As she left, I thanked God for her and remembered she was my child.

When my wife and I are gone, our children will get the few earthly things that we have. Our children are heirs. You are an heir of God through Christ. You receive the gift of eternal life from God as God's child and God's heir.

WEEK ONE: TO KNOW MYSELF

Day 4 ✷ I Am Crowned with Glory and Honor

BIBLE VERSE: Yet you made them inferior only to yourself;
you crowned them with glory and honor.

— Psalm 8:5

PRAYER: O God, when you made me, you made me high in your order. I am above every animal and plant. I am just below your angels. I am crowned with glory and honor.

But here I am in prison, locked up and stripped of all dignity and respect. Here I am treated like a nothing.

But with you I am crowned with honor and glory. Help me remember, O God, who I am with you. In the name of Jesus, our Lord. Amen.

THOUGHT FOR THE DAY: There is an order of being. First, there is God: the Father, the Son, and the Holy Spirit—all in one. Second, there are the angels. Human beings are third, and fourth are animals and plants. Humanity is above all other animals and only a little lower than the angels.

I am a high creature, made by God, and crowned with glory and honor.

WEEK ONE: TO KNOW MYSELF

Day 5 ✷ God's Ways Are Better Than My Ways

BIBLE VERSE: "My thoughts," says the LORD, "are not
like yours,
and my ways are different from
yours.
As high as the heavens are above
the earth,
so high are my ways and thoughts
above yours."
— Isaiah 55:8-9

PRAYER: You tell me, Lord, that your ways are better than my ways. You tell me that your thoughts are better than my thoughts.

But I have been dumb not to believe you. I have gone my way and not your way. I have had my thoughts, not your thoughts—and here I am.

Now, Lord, I want to try your ways. I want to have some of your thoughts. My life is in a mess because I followed my ways and not your ways. Help me, Lord, to start following your ways. In Jesus' name. Amen.

THOUGHT FOR THE DAY: You were made in the image of God. You are a child of God. But you can't live in the Lord if you just follow your own will. Why? Because God's ways are better than your ways. Your ways get you into trouble. God's ways lead you to salvation and to victory over sin and temptation.

WEEK ONE: TO KNOW MYSELF

Day 6 ✷ I Have Gone Astray

BIBLE VERSE: All of us were like sheep that were lost,
each of us going his own way.
But the LORD made the punishment
fall on him,
the punishment all of us deserved.
— Isaiah 53:6

PRAYER: O Lord, we have gone astray. We have gone our own ways rather than your ways. We have turned to alcohol, to drugs, to stealing, lying, adultery, and hatred. These are not your ways, O Lord.

And we have gotten into trouble. We have strayed from your presence. We have been locked up, hurt, separated. We have been cast out and cast down by others.

But you say in your word that you laid our sins on your servant. Forgive me, God, and bring me home to you. In the name of Jesus. Amen.

THOUGHT FOR THE DAY: A sheep must follow its shepherd to be secure. When a sheep leaves the shepherd and goes astray, it gets lost and hungry, and it is often killed. A lost sheep is often in trouble.

We, like sheep, get lost and in danger when we stray from the shepherd, our Lord. And we have all done this. We are like the sheep gone astray, and we need to get back to our shepherd, God.

Week One: To Know Myself

Day 7 ✵ I Am a Sinner

Bible Verse: Everyone has sinned and is far away from God's saving presence.

— Romans 3:23

Prayer: O God, I am a sinner. I have done my way instead of your way. I have violated your laws, many of them. I have missed the mark of your purpose for my life. I have loved myself more than I have loved you. I have hurt other people.

And I have separated myself from your presence, O God. Forgive me. I want to come back to you. In the name of Jesus. Amen.

Thought for the Day: I am a sinner. You are a sinner. All of us are sinners. To sin is to do our own will instead of God's will. To sin is to violate God's law. To sin is to miss the mark of God's purpose for our lives. To sin is to hurt other people and ourselves.

Sin separates us from God and turns us toward hell. We *are* sinners. We need God to save us.

WEEK TWO: TO KNOW GOD

Day 1 ✷ I Need to Know God

BIBLE VERSE: Listen to me, LORD, and answer me,
for I am helpless and weak.
— Psalms 86:1

PRAYER: O Lord, only you know how poor and needy I really am. I am locked away from people I love. I even feel I am away from you, O Lord. I need to know you care. I need to know you will help me. I need to know you as my Lord.

I don't want to be a stranger to you, Lord. I want you to be my friend. I need you to listen to my story. I need to know you care.

I know, O Lord, you will hear me and make yourself known to me. I believe you are hearing me right now. I pray you will let me know you are here. In the name of Jesus. Amen.

THOUGHT FOR THE DAY: We are each poor in many ways. In prison, we are poor in spirit, for we have lost our freedom. But God hears us and listens to our cries. God hears our prayers. God knows we are poor in many ways and that our needs are great.

God does hear us and knows us. And God lets *us* know him!

WEEK TWO: TO KNOW GOD

Day 2 ✵ I Will Call upon Thee

BIBLE VERSE: I call to you in times of trouble,
because you answer my prayers.
— Psalm 86:7

PRAYER: O God, I want to know you. I haven't known you very much in the past. I have passed you by. I have thought mainly of myself. But now, O God, I really want to know who you are. I want to feel your presence. I want to know you are here with me.

This is a time of trouble for me. You have said it's all right to call on you when I am in trouble. So God, I call on you now in my day of trouble. And I know you will answer me, according to your word.

Help me know you are here and that you care. In the name of Jesus. Amen.

THOUGHT FOR THE DAY: God is everywhere. God is as close as the air you breathe. You can call upon God. God will make himself known to you by the Holy Spirit.

WEEK TWO: TO KNOW GOD

Day 3 ✷ God Is Just

BIBLE VERSE: Let justice flow like a stream, and righteousness like a river that never goes dry.

— Amos 5:24

PRAYER: God of our ancestors, you are a just God. You are the beginning of all justice. I praise you, God, and worship you as a God of justice. Help me know what you expect of me as I live in your world.

God, I have not always been just and fair in my dealings with other people and with you. Forgive me for that, O God. Teach me to do the right thing each day. Let justice flow like a stream in my own life, that others may see right actions and attitudes in the way I live.

Lead me to do the right thing in relation to other people, to those around me. In Jesus' name I pray. Amen.

THOUGHT FOR THE DAY: God is the God of justice and right actions. God does not punish the innocent nor reward the sinner. And God knows all about us. As God of justice, God expects us to be just and to seek to do the right thing as we live around other people.

WEEK TWO: TO KNOW GOD

Day 4 ✷ God Is Good

BIBLE VERSE: You are good to us and forgiving,
full of constant love for all who pray
to you.

— Psalm 86:5

PRAYER: Lord, your word tells me you are good. You show mercy. I need to know your goodness, Lord. I need your mercy because I have not done your will in my life.

Lord, I want to go to heaven when I die. But I also want you in my heart here while I live. I know you have plenty of mercy because your word teaches me that you do.

I call on you, Lord, to show mercy to me according to your word. Amen.

THOUGHT FOR THE DAY: God is good. God is ready to forgive you. God has plenty of mercy for you if you call on him. How can God show justice and mercy both? God is our heavenly Parent.

WEEK TWO: TO KNOW GOD

Day 5 ✷ God Is Love

BIBLE VERSE: Dear friends, let us love one another, because love comes from God. Whoever loves is a child of God and knows God. Whoever does not love does not know God, for God is love.

— 1 John 4:7-8.

PRAYER: O God, help me know you by loving you and by loving others. You say in your word that if we love you and others, we are born of God.

You say that you are love. Yet so many people today hate one another. It's hard, God, to love others. It's hard even to love you. Bring me to the point of loving others, God. With your spirit, conquer hate in my heart and teach me to love. For you are pure love. In the name of Jesus, who loved us and gave himself for us. Amen.

THOUGHT FOR THE DAY: To know God is to know that God is love. Jesus loved people, and he showed us what God is like. A fellow inmate knew inspection was due and he saw my bunk wasn't made right. He came over and made it right for me. He said, "I just wanted to help you out." He loved God and had learned in his spirit to love those around him.

Week Two: To Know God

Day 6 ✸ God in Jesus

Bible Verse: Jesus answered, "For a long time I have been with you all; yet you do not know me, Philip? Whoever has seen me has seen the Father. Why, then, do you say, 'Show us the Father'? Do you not believe, Philip, that I am in the Father and the Father is in me? The words that I have spoken to you," Jesus said to his disciples, "do not come from me. The Father, who remains in me, does his own work."

— John 14:9-10

Prayer: God, I have often wanted to see you. I have longed to see your face, to hear your voice, to touch your hand. But I never have.

Now I learn that Jesus was like you. As Jesus talked, you talked. As Jesus acted, you acted. Help me to know Jesus that I may know you.

Jesus healed and loved and forgave. You do these things now, God, through the Holy Spirit. And for this I praise you. In the name of Jesus. Amen.

Thought for the Day: Philip wanted to see God the Father. He asked Jesus to show him God because that was all he needed. Jesus said that whoever had seen *him* had seen the Father.

Do you want to know God? Then read the life of Jesus in Matthew, Mark, Luke, and John. You will see God in Jesus.

WEEK TWO: TO KNOW GOD

Day 7 ✷ I Can Know God in Prison

BIBLE VERSE: While I was still imprisoned in the palace courtyard, the LORD told me to tell Ebedmelech the Ethiopian that the LORD Almighty, the God of Israel, had said, "Just as I said I would, I am going to bring upon this city destruction and not prosperity. And when this happens, you will be there to see it."

—Jeremiah 39:15-16

PRAYER: O Lord, thank you that no bars can shut out your word. No keys can lock out your word. No walls can block out your word. No fences can stop your word. Thank you, God! Amen.

THOUGHT FOR THE DAY: When a person is in prison, it is hard to receive most anything. Mail is late. It's hard to receive phone calls, newspapers, and visitors.

But it is not hard to receive the word of the Lord! You can get a Bible if you don't have one. And God's word comes to you in prayer. Thank God that God's word comes to persons in prison.

You can know God in prison! You need to know God in prison!

WEEK THREE: TO KNOW GOD'S LOVE

Day 1 ✸ God Loves Me

BIBLE VERSE: For God loved the world so much that he gave his only Son, so that everyone who believes in him may not die but have eternal life.

—John 3:16

PRAYER: O God, how can I believe you love me that much? Others say I'm a dirty "con," an old "thing." But you say I'm a child of yours—and you love me!

O God, I come to you now. Just as I am I come to you. I don't wear a mask. I don't pretend. I come as I am. Let me know that you love me. In the name of Jesus. Amen.

THOUGHT FOR THE DAY: Believing is your part for eternal life. But love is God's part. You believe in God. God loves you. God loves you so much that God gave his only son for you! I could not do that. I love my children more than anyone else except my wife. I could not give one of my children for someone else's sake. But God did! God gave God's only son because God loves you that much!

You are not "an old thing." You are not a dirty "con." You are not a "no-good bum." You are a child of God whom God loves! Hallelujah!

WEEK THREE: TO KNOW GOD'S LOVE

Day 2 ✷ I Can Know God's Love

BIBLE VERSE: Yes, may you come to know his love—although it can never be fully known—and so be completely filled with the very nature of God.

— Ephesians 3:19

PRAYER: God, I long to know your love for me. At times I'm not sure you really love me. I get lonely. I feel forgotten and forsaken. Yet you say in your word that you *are* love. You say you loved me enough to die for me. I know that you do love me, Lord, and that you know who I am. I pray that I may know your love for me. In the name of Jesus. Amen.

THOUGHT FOR THE DAY: Raymond was working on a car when a motor fell on his foot. The motor tore his foot and took off his toenail. The foot was bloody, dirty, and painful. I bathed it, disinfected the cut, bandaged it, and taped it. Others watched. He said, "Why did you do that?" I said, "In the name of Jesus, to help your foot, and then to let you know that someone cares." Raymond's father had disappeared. His mother had rejected him. But he later came to know God. You too can know the love of God!

WEEK THREE: TO KNOW GOD'S LOVE

Day 3 ✹ God Always Loves Me

BIBLE VERSE: We ourselves know and believe the love which God has for us. God is love, and those who live in love live in union with God and God lives in union with them.

— 1 John 4:16

PRAYER: Lord, I do not understand why I suffer. Yet I know you love me, Lord. Help me understand more fully your love, even through the punishment that has come to me. Help me know you as a God of love. In the name of Jesus. Amen.

THOUGHT FOR THE DAY: How can it be that God loves us and yet we suffer punishment? In our suffering, we can come to know God in a very special way. Very few people in the world suffer as completely and as long as those in prison. No one else knows the suffering prison brings. We can know God in our suffering if we turn to God in prayer and in faith.

We must be careful, however, not to ascribe our punishment and suffering to God. Some well-meaning people can say that; yet God does not make us suffer. God loves us.

Through your suffering, you can come to know God in a completely new way. God's love will come to you.

WEEK THREE: TO KNOW GOD'S LOVE

Day 4 ✷ Christ Gave Himself for Me

Bible Verse: Your life must be controlled by love, just as Christ loved us and gave his life for us as a sweet-smelling offering and sacrifice that pleases God.

— Ephesians 5:2

PRAYER: O God, you gave your Son for me, an offering of love for my sins! Nothing I do can atone for my sins. Nothing I do can make up for them. Only *you* can do that.

Being in prison makes nothing right, Lord. Serving time corrects no mistake, rights no wrong. And so I come to you in repentance and faith, knowing you love me. Thank you, God, for your love freely given. I do not deserve it. In the name of Jesus. Amen.

THOUGHT FOR THE DAY: I once saw an altar used for human sacrifice in old Israel. People were placed on the altar in ancient times and killed as a sacrifice to God.

Today people sometimes think that when a person is sent to prison—or executed—that "things are made right." Not so. The only things that can "make right" a wrong are the sacrifice of Christ for sins, our belief in Christ, and our repentance. Christ is the sacrifice for our sins!

Week Three: To Know God's Love

Day 5 ✷ God Loves in Suffering

Bible Verse: Because of our sins he was wounded,
beaten because of the evil we did.
We are healed by the punishment he suffered,
made whole by the blows he received.
— Isaiah 53:5

Prayer: O God, how much do you love me and all of your people? Enough to allow Jesus to die for us. Enough to allow Jesus to suffer for us. You love us enough to allow Jesus to be beaten and insulted for us.

Your son went to the cross, Lord, as an offering for our sins. Your son even died to replace our death for our sins.

Thank you, God! Thank you for your love. I don't understand it. I don't deserve it. But I accept it as freely given from you! Amen.

Thought for the Day: When I was suffering in prison, my sons said, "I wish I could serve for you, Dad." They meant it too. Jesus did that for you—he suffered for you because he loves you. He was wounded for your sins. He was beaten for you and me although he was innocent. The whip made stripes on his body. With his stripes you are healed, forgiven of your sins, and made whole.

Week Three: To Know God's Love

Day 6 ✵ Christ Became a Prisoner for Me

Bible Verse: He was arrested and sentenced and
led off to die,
and no one cared about his fate.
He was put to death for the sins of
our people.
— Isaiah 53:8

Prayer: O God, your only son became a prisoner. He suffered pain, humiliation, rejection, and death for me and for all your children.

I want to know your love. And I know that if you allowed Jesus to become a prisoner for me and die for me, you must love me and all of your children everywhere!

Lord, your son did not deserve to suffer the pain and humiliation of being accused, arrested, tried, and convicted. Yet he suffered the final and ultimate pain for us. I don't deserve that, Lord. Praise your name for your great mercy! Amen.

Thought for the Day: Jesus Christ—the Son of God—was a prisoner! He was accused, arrested, tried, convicted, and executed. He died as a prisoner—all for you and me!

For our sins Jesus was stricken. He became a prisoner for you. He suffered and even died for you!

All that we might live in eternity.

WEEK THREE: TO KNOW GOD'S LOVE

Day 7 ✷ God's Love Is Permanent

BIBLE VERSE: For I am certain that nothing can separate us from his love: neither death nor life, neither angels nor other heavenly rulers or powers, neither the present nor the future, neither the world above nor the world below—there is nothing in all creation that will ever be able to separate us from the love of God which is ours through Christ Jesus our Lord.

— Romans 8:38-39

PRAYER: O God, no walls can shut out your love. No gates can keep away your concern. Nothing can separate me from your love, Lord—nothing!

And now I pray that your love abides with me here and in this place, now and forever. Amen!

THOUGHT FOR THE DAY: One day as I was marching back to Unit 29 from lunch, I looked up and saw a sparrow taking a twig to a crack in the wall. She was building a nest. The same building that was my prison was her home. I thought of the words of Jesus, "Not one sparrow falls to the ground without your Father's consent" (Matt. 10:29). I knew that the same God who watched over that sparrow was watching over me too!

WEEK FOUR: FOR REPENTANCE

Day 1 ✵ Ask God to Take Over

BIBLE VERSE: Turn away from all the evil you are doing, and don't let your sin destroy you.

— Ezekiel 18:30

PRAYER: Lord, I have been on the wrong road, headed toward hell. I want to turn around and go the right way. I repent of all my wrong living. I turn to you. I want to go your way with my life.

Lord, while I have gone the wrong way, I have hurt other people and myself. I want to live for you, Lord. I turn now to you. In Jesus' name. Amen.

THOUGHT FOR THE DAY: Once I entered a four-lane highway heading the wrong way. I saw a big red sign that read Wrong Way. I turned around right then and headed back. We get on the wrong road in life. To repent means to turn around and go the *right* way—the way of God.

WEEK FOUR: FOR REPENTANCE

Day 2 ✷ Face Up to Sin

BIBLE VERSE: I recognize my faults;
I am always conscious of my sins.
— Psalm 51:3

PRAYER: Dear God, you demand right living. I have lived wrongly. All your people have done wrong. I face up to my sins, O God. Some of the things I have done wrong are: [here, name your sins to God]. I admit these to you, O God, and do not hide them any longer.

You are God, holy and pure. I am a sinner, lowly and impure. My sin is ever before me, and now I face up to it before you, O God. In Jesus' name. Amen.

THOUGHT FOR THE DAY: David, who wrote this psalm, had committed both adultery and murder. He was God's man who had done wrong. He had separated himself from God. But David faced his sin, repented of his sin, and was forgiven by God. (Read Psalm 51.)

We too must face our sins in order to repent. What are the sins of your life? Face up to them as David did.

WEEK FOUR: FOR REPENTANCE

Day 3 ✻ Repent or Die

BIBLE VERSE: I tell you that if you do not turn from your sins, you will all die as they did.

— Luke 13:3

PRAYER: You have told us, God, to repent or die. I know you mean what you say and say what you mean. I have been going in the wrong direction. I have not followed you. My sin has led me here—and away from you, God.

Right now I turn to you, O God. I turn away from my sin. I plan to follow you, God, where you lead me. I am sorry for my sins. Lead me where you want me to go. In the name of Jesus. Amen.

THOUGHT FOR THE DAY: Some men came to Jesus. They told him of people who had been killed by the governor. Jesus said that those who had been killed were not greater sinners than those who were telling about it. Jesus told them that they too could die unless they repented.

Sin is serious. Its penalty is spiritual death—unless we repent.

WEEK FOUR: FOR REPENTANCE

Day 4 ✷ Line Up with God's Will

BIBLE VERSE: May your Kingdom come;
may your will be done on earth as it is
in heaven.

— Matthew 6:10

PRAYER: God, your will is better than my will. Your plans are better than my plans. My will gets me into trouble. Your will, your plans keep me out of trouble.

Help me, O God, look for your plans. Help me follow your plans. Help me do your will, not mine. I truly want to line up with your will, O God. In the name of Jesus. Amen.

THOUGHT FOR THE DAY: When God made you, God gave you a mind of your own. You can choose the way of your life. But God has a mind and a will. God's will is better for you than your will.

When you line up your will with God's will, you are headed toward victory and success. You are headed toward right living in the Lord.

WEEK FOUR: FOR REPENTANCE

Day 5 ✵ Be Converted

BIBLE VERSE: Repent, then, and turn to God, so that he will forgive your sins. If you do, times of spiritual strength will come from the Lord, and he will send Jesus, who is the Messiah he has already chosen for you.

— Acts 3:19-20

PRAYER: O God, I strayed far away from you. I started hating others. I used your name in vain. I hurt other people. Now, O God, I turn back to you. I love you, Lord.

You say in your word that my sins will be forgiven. Thank you, Lord. You say I will receive spiritual strength. I repent and turn to you, Lord. In the name of Jesus. Amen.

THOUGHT FOR THE DAY: Robert stood before thirty other inmates in a prayer service. He said, "I got away from God. I started cussing. I hated everybody. I made up my mind to kill a man. But I used to go to church and sing in church. Now I have turned around. I have come back to Jesus." Robert did come back to Jesus. He had stopped cursing. He led the singing for the prayer meeting. He forgave others.

WEEK FOUR: FOR REPENTANCE

Day 6 ✺ Get Straight with God

BIBLE VERSE: Let the wicked leave their way of life
and change their way of thinking.
Let them turn to the LORD, our God;
he is merciful and quick to forgive.
— Isaiah 55:7

PRAYER: Lord of the truth, I forsake my ways of the past. I turn my back on lying and deception. In the name of Jesus, I cast out falsehoods. I return to you, O Lord, and to your ways. I leave my own thoughts behind and turn to your thoughts.

You say in your word you will have mercy on me and pardon me. I claim now your mercy and your pardon. In Jesus' name. Amen.

THOUGHT FOR THE DAY: Lying and deception are at the root of every sin. I remember the peace that came to me when I decided to stop lying and to live the truth. The strength of God came to me. Even though the truth brought hard results, God pardoned me and had mercy on me. Praise God!

WEEK FOUR: FOR REPENTANCE

Day 7 ✷ Pray for All to Repent

BIBLE VERSE: He [the Lord] does not want anyone to be destroyed, but wants all to turn away from their sins.

— 2 Peter 3:9

PRAYER: O God, I pray not only for myself, but for all your children. I pray for everyone to come to repentance. All of us have sinned: lawyers, preachers, teachers, officers, everyone. I pray for all, O Lord, to come to repentance.

I know that you love everyone and do not want any of your children to die in their sins. In the name of Jesus. Amen.

THOUGHT FOR THE DAY: Who needs to repent? Who needs to turn to the Lord? Thieves? Murderers? Liars? *Yes, but not just people who have openly done wrong. Everybody needs to repent and turn to the Lord!*

The most deadly sin of all is pride because pride makes us blind to our need for repentance. We are being proud when we think only *other* people need to repent.

The Lord doesn't want *any* person to perish. God yearns for all to come to repentance.

WEEK FIVE: FOR SALVATION

Day 1 ✷ Salvation Today

BIBLE VERSE: Hear what God says:

"When the time came for me to show you favor,
    I heard you;
when the day arrived for me to save you,
    I helped you."
Listen! This is the hour to receive God's favor; today is the day to be saved!

— 2 Corinthians 6:2

PRAYER: I have put off my salvation, Lord. I have waited almost too long. Now I come to you wanting to be saved. Lord, I give my life and heart to you right now, in this terrible place and in this hard time.

You say in your word that whoever comes to you, you will not cast out. I come to you, Lord. I know you accept me and save me. In the name of Jesus. Amen.

THOUGHT FOR THE DAY: The chaplain had just left. Charlie said, "I will become a Christian when I leave this place. You can't be a Christian in here." I said, "I won't argue with you, but the Bible says, 'Today is the day to be saved.' "

If salvation is good, the sooner it comes, the better. If it is bad, it is better never to have it. Salvation is not only good, it is necessary for eternal life and for living as a Christian here and now.

WEEK FIVE: FOR SALVATION

Day 2 ✸ Complete Salvation

BIBLE VERSE: How, then, shall we escape if we pay no attention to such a great salvation? The Lord himself first announced this salvation, and those who heard him proved to us that it is true.

— Hebrews 2:3

PRAYER: Christ Jesus, your salvation is great. I want to know you as my personal Savior. I want to know I am saved completely. I know if I am not saved, I shall not escape hell to come or hell here on earth right now!

I accept you as my Lord and Savior, Jesus. I believe in you as God's Son and my Savior. Amen.

THOUGHT FOR THE DAY: One night we were having a prayer meeting in the cellblock. I was preaching, but no one was reponding. I stopped and said, "Let's pray." Several of the inmates began to pray. Through the guidance of the Holy Spirit, I felt, "Someone needs to be saved." The Spirit led me to preach on salvation from Acts 16, where Paul and Silas convert a jailer and his family to belief in the Lord Jesus. At the end I gave an invitation. Two inmates, Walter and Charles, came to accept Jesus as Savior. They have grown in Christ since then.

Our salvation is truly great in the Lord.

Week Five: For Salvation

Day 3 ✸ How Am I Saved?

Bible Verse: For it is by God's grace that you have been saved through faith.

— Ephesians 2:8

Prayer: I believe in you, Lord Jesus. You are God's only son. I believe you lived, died, rose from the dead, and now come to us through the Holy Spirit. I believe you are the Savior of the world and are God's son.

I know I am saved because God's grace comes when one has faith. This is in the word. I am saved by God's grace! In your name. Amen.

Thought for the Day: How can we be saved? How can we be sure we are saved? The Bible says we are saved by having faith in Jesus Christ. We are saved when we trust in and follow Jesus Christ.

Grace is God's gift. It means God gives us salvation. We cannot earn it. We cannot work for it. We do not deserve it. God *gives* it to us. God gives us salvation when we have faith in Jesus Christ as the Son of God.

WEEK FIVE: FOR SALVATION

Day 4 ✷ Salvation and Strength

BIBLE VERSE: Then I heard a loud voice in heaven saying, "Now God's salvation has come! Now God has shown his power as King! Now his Messiah has shown his authority! For the one who stood before our God and accused believers day and night has been thrown out of heaven."

— Revelation 12:10

PRAYER: You can save anybody, Lord. You can change anybody. You can save me. You can change me. You can give me your strength and your salvation. Save me, Lord. Give me your strength and your salvation through your Son Jesus Christ. In Jesus' name. Amen.

THOUGHT FOR THE DAY: James is big and tall and strong. He went to jail because he cut somebody in the face. James was hard to get along with. He had a hot temper. One night we were talking. I said, "James, are you a Christian?" He said, "No." I said, "Would you like to accept Jesus and be saved?" He said, "I sure would." We prayed a prayer of salvation for him. I laid hands on his head. He gave his heart to Jesus. He now reads the Bible each day and *lives* the change that has come over him. He will get out of jail soon. His nature was changed so that now he is gentle and kind to others because he is strong in the Lord.

WEEK FIVE: FOR SALVATION

Day 5 ✸ Restoring the Joy of Salvation

BIBLE VERSE: Give me again the joy that comes from
your salvation,
and make me willing to obey you.
— Psalm 51:12

PRAYER: God, you are all joy, all love, all power. Clean up my heart and my life, Lord. Take away my sin. I haven't smiled in quite a while. I want to smile again. I want to laugh once more. I want to feel your presence with me, Lord.

I once had the joy of salvation and lost it. I went my own way and not your way. Now, Lord, I come back to you. I claim the joy of your salvation. In the name of Jesus. Amen.

THOUGHT FOR THE DAY: We were in the hot dining room one summer night. We were singing, "I will rejoice, I will rejoice!" The joy of salvation was there. When we finished singing, One-Eye said, "I want to say a word." He told us how he loved Jesus. He said, "I didn't know the Lord until last year. I accepted Jesus and now he lives in my heart." The joy of salvation was in the heart of One-Eye.

WEEK FIVE: FOR SALVATION

Day 6 ✷ Save My Family

BIBLE VERSE: Believe in the Lord Jesus, and you will be saved—you and your family.

—Acts 16:31

PRAYER: I want to be saved, Lord. And I want my family to be saved too. I believe in you, Lord Jesus, and I accept you as Lord and Savior.

But sometimes it is hard to believe. Sometimes I confess that I am like the man who said to you, "I do have faith, but not enough. Help me have more!" (Mark 9:24)

Save my spirit, Lord. Save my house and my family, according to God's word. May the love of God come down upon us. In your name I pray. Amen.

THOUGHT FOR THE DAY: Larry was talking with me. He and Elizabeth, his wife, had been crying. He had been on a pass. Another man had called her. Larry wanted me to pray for him and for his wife. I did. I asked him if Elizabeth was a Christian. He said, "No." We prayed for her. We prayed that God would save both of them and their household.

His home life still isn't settled, but Larry has found salvation through his belief in Christ.

WEEK FIVE: FOR SALVATION

Day 7 ✷ The Purposes of God

BIBLE VERSE: Then I will teach sinners your commands,
and they will turn back to you.
— Psalm 51:13

PRAYER: I want to bring someone to you, Lord. I am not content just to have salvation myself. I want others to have it.

Give me the courage, Lord, to teach sinners about you. Open my mouth so sinners will be converted to you. Use me in this place to be your witness. Wherever I am, help me be your witness to convert your children to you. Save me from being timid, or afraid to speak for you.

Give me the joy of salvation that it may overflow from my life to the lives of others. In Jesus' name. Amen.

THOUGHT FOR THE DAY: When Jesus Christ lives in our hearts, we want to share him with others. Christ brings joy to us that we cannot contain. We *want* to witness to others for him.

Walter, who had come to know the Lord, got up one night in a prayer meeting and told of his conversion. That same night after he had spoken, three more accepted Jesus and became Christians.

WEEK SIX: FOR TRUST IN GOD

Day 1 ✷ I Trust in God

BIBLE VERSE: I come to you, LORD, for protection;
never let me be defeated.
You are a righteous God;
save me, I pray!
— Psalm 31:1

PRAYER: O Lord, you are with me at all times. You are with me even now in this awful place. You, Lord, are my God. You are my rock. I can even feel that you are here, O Lord.

I can be a Christian here in this confining and grinding place. You alone can save me, Lord. I cannot save myself. Other people cannot save me. You alone can save me.

I put my trust in you, O Lord. I give my life to you. I trust in you completely. In the name of Jesus. Amen.

THOUGHT FOR THE DAY: Cedric said to me, "I'll be a Christian when I get out of prison. But right now I'm gonna do things my way. You can't be a Christian in this place." He is still in prison and was sent to a harder camp because of his general attitude.

Where is your trust? Put your trust in God. God will not let you down. God will not lie to you. God will not deceive you. Trust in God!

Week Six: For Trust in God

Day 2 ✵ I Trust in God—Not in Myself

Bible Verses: We felt that the death sentence had been passed on us. But this happened so that we should rely, not on ourselves, but only on God, who raises the dead.

—2 Corinthians 1:9

Trust in the Lord with all your heart. Never rely on what you think you know.

—Proverbs 3:5

Prayer: God, I come to you today. You have the answers, not me. You know all things, Lord. You even know what is best for me when I do not know myself. You are the Lord God! I am only me. God, I place my trust in you, not in myself. Lead my life. Guide and direct me in your paths. Amen.

Thought for the Day: Sero, a young prisoner, came to me one night and said, "I want you to pray for me." I said, "Sure, what about?" He said, "My girl has quit writing me and in her last letter she was cold to me. I'm afraid she's breaking up with me." I said, "What do you want me to pray?" He said, "That she will still love me." I said, "I cannot pray that. It has to be right for her too. But I will pray that you trust in God for your happiness and hers too." We prayed together and he began to trust God to bring him peace.

WEEK SIX: FOR TRUST IN GOD

Day 3 ✷ I Trust in God—Not in Others

BIBLE VERSE: It is better to trust in the LORD
than to depend on people.
— Psalm 118:8

PRAYER: Lord, it is so easy to trust people and forget you. You can do all things, Lord. You never lie. You never forget. You can watch over my family. You can bring me out of prison.

Lord, I trust my life to you—to you and you alone. Save me from placing my trust in other people when it belongs in you. Others will fail to keep their word; they will betray and forget me. You do none of these things, Lord. I trust you! Amen.

THOUGHT FOR THE DAY: Did you put all your eggs in one basket? Did you trust your lawyer, your friends, your "connections"? If so, you made a big mistake.

Put your trust *first* in the Lord. God will never lie to you. All things are possible with God. God can bring you out of prison. People forget—but not God. People lie—but not God. People are weak; God is strong. Trust God!

WEEK SIX: FOR TRUST IN GOD

Day 4 ✷ I Trust in God for Victory

BIBLE VERSE: In you, my God, I trust.
Save me from the shame of defeat;
don't let my enemies gloat over me!
— Psalm 25:2

PRAYER: My God, I trust in you. I place my life in your hands for victory. Keep me from wanting to get even with those who have hurt me, God. Help me be your witness. Help me stay away from the sources of evil and sin.

Make my witness strong for you, God. Let me trust in you for all things. You have my life, O God. I do trust in you. Amen.

THOUGHT FOR THE DAY: You have a fight on your hands. You can follow the ways of God that lead to victory, or you can follow the ways of evil and sin. Sin will ruin you. It destroys your life. Sin is your real enemy—not other people.

God can help you beat sin and evil. God will help you *if* you trust in God. Give your heart to God because God can defeat sin and evil in your life. Trust in God!

Week Six: For Trust in God

Day 5 ✵ I Trust in God When I'm Burdened

Bible Verse: Leave your troubles with the Lord,
and he will defend you;
he never lets honest men be defeated.
— Psalm 55:22

Prayer: Lord God, I don't have a broken bone. But I do have a broken heart and a broken spirit. I feel I cannot make it through all of this. I worry about my family. I worry about my health. I worry about getting out.

Lord, I cast my burdens on you. I give to you my broken heart and broken spirit. They are too heavy for me to bear alone.

Lift me up, O God. I trust in you and you alone. I pray in your name. Amen.

Thought for the Day: Wendell had a broken leg. The cast was heavy, and he hobbled around prison on crutches. He could not take a shower. He had to march to meals through the rain on crutches. Yet he always smiled and had a good word. I asked him, "How do you do it?" He replied, "I gave the broken leg to the Lord." Wendell is now out of his cast and the smile of the Lord is still with him. Cast your burdens on the Lord.

WEEK SIX: FOR TRUST IN GOD

Day 6 ✷ I Trust in God When I'm Afraid

BIBLE VERSE: Do not be afraid—I am with you!
I am your God—let nothing terrify you!
I will make you strong and help you;
I will protect you and save you.
— Isaiah 41:10

PRAYER: I get afraid, Lord. I don't know what will happen to me. I get afraid for my family. But you tell me not to fear. When I get afraid and weak, Lord, remind me of your promise. Teach me not to be afraid. Teach me the way and the habit of trusting in you.

I will give my life to you and trust in you. I will not be afraid, for you are with me, O God. You are my God. You give me strength. I pray in your holy name. Amen.

THOUGHT FOR THE DAY: Before I preached my first sermon, I was frozen with fear. My throat almost closed with fright. A friend gave me a piece of paper with this scribble on it: "Isaiah 41:10." I looked it up. I knew that God was with me and that I had no need to be afraid.

Are you afraid down deep? Are you afraid of something or of someone? Are you afraid of the future?

Trust in God. *God is with you!*

WEEK SIX: FOR TRUST IN GOD

Day 7 ✸ I Trust in God All the Time

BIBLE VERSE: I've lost all hope, so what if God
kills me?
I am going to state my case to him.
— Job 13:15

PRAYER: O God, I have lost so much. My freedom. My job. My friends. Maybe even some of my family. But God, I have not lost my faith.

No matter what happens to me, O God, I will trust in you. Even if things don't work out as I want them to, I will trust in you. My trust will not go. Even until I die, O God, I will trust in you. In the name of Jesus. Amen.

THOUGHT FOR THE DAY: Job had it made. Lots of land. A big herd of cows. Thousands of sheep. A big house. Plenty of money. Lots of servants. A wife. Children. Friends. A strong body. What could happen to a man with everything? He lost it all. Everything he had—everything but his faith.

Then it all came back—and more.

Have you lost it all? Keep your faith and your trust in God. Trust in God *all* of the time!

WEEK SEVEN: TO FORGIVE OTHERS

Day 1 ✷ Friends Who "Made Me Do It"

BIBLE VERSE: Then Peter came to Jesus and asked, "Lord, if my brother keeps on sinning against me, how many times do I have to forgive him? Seven times?" "No, not seven times," answered Jesus, "but seventy times seven."

— Matthew 18:21-22

PRAYER: I am the one who got myself into trouble, Lord. Nobody made me do it. But sometimes I feel like someone else made me do it.

I fell in with the wrong group and they influenced me. But the actions were mine. I need to forgive these people, Lord, for I often blame them for what happened. I do forgive them, each one of them in the name of the Lord Jesus. Amen.

THOUGHT FOR THE DAY: Jesus taught us to forgive others so that God will forgive us. Jesus told Peter to forgive others "seventy times seven"—that is, any number of times. We need to forgive others over and over.

Walter told me, "I wouldn't be here in prison if it wasn't for Frank and the others. They got me to go with them and got me into it that night." He felt hardness in his heart toward Frank and his friends because they had convinced him to go with them the night of the robbery. We prayed about it, and Walter forgave them.

WEEK SEVEN: TO FORGIVE OTHERS

Day 2 ✵ The Judge, The District Attorney, The Arresting Officer

BIBLE VERSE: You have heard that it was said, "Love your friends, hate your enemies." But now I tell you: love your enemies and pray for those who persecute you.

— Matthew 5:43-44

PRAYER: People have hurt me, God. The officer arrested me. The district attorney prosecuted me. The judge sentenced me. Others have cursed me. Friends have left me, God.

I need your grace, God, to allow me to forgive them. I cannot do this on my own. They did not know how much it hurt; and when it was over, they went home with their families while I went to jail.

In the name of Jesus, who forgave, I too forgive those who hurt me so much. In the name of Jesus. Amen.

THOUGHT FOR THE DAY: Jesus set the example for us in forgiving other people. No one ever had as much to forgive as Jesus did. He was innocent. The Pharisees accused him. The Romans put him to death. Friends left him. Soldiers cursed him and spat on him. He was in pain, shock, and agony. Yet he *forgave* those who did these things to him. He set the example for us.

WEEK SEVEN: TO FORGIVE OTHERS

Day 3 ✷ Relatives Who Let Me Down

BIBLE VERSE: Lord, hear us. Lord, forgive us. Lord, listen to us, and act! In order that everyone will know that you are God, do not delay! This city and these people are yours.

— Daniel 9:19

PRAYER: Not all of my relatives have helped me, God. Some don't care. Others have dropped me. This is hard to take, Lord. You know that it is. The way they have treated me makes me feel so alone.

But Lord, you have taught me to forgive everybody—including those who forget me and do not come to see me. I do forgive them, Lord, in the name of Jesus. Amen.

THOUGHT FOR THE DAY: Raymond was very excited. He paced around smiling. "What's up, Raymond?" I asked. "My mom's coming to see me. She lives in West Virginia, and she's coming to see my sister this weekend and she will come to see me." "That's great," I said. Saturday came. Raymond was clean and had on a fresh shirt. He waited. He waited through the whole day. That night he was weeping. She came to see his sister, but she did not come to see him. The next day Raymond's anger came out; he got into a fight.

Relatives don't always support a person in prison. Pray for forgiveness for them too.

WEEK SEVEN: TO FORGIVE OTHERS

Day 4 ✷ Victims

BIBLE VERSE: And when you stand and pray, forgive anything you may have against anyone, so that your Father in heaven will forgive the wrongs you have done.

— Mark 11:25

PRAYER: I don't know why I don't like these people so much, Lord, but I don't. Sometimes I feel like I really hate them—the people I hurt, that is, my victims. They didn't do anything to deserve what happened to them, but I still don't like them and that's not right. Somehow I feel that I must forgive them.

Lord, at this time I forgive all the people I have mistreated. Something inside me made me mistreat them. I know I must forgive them too, in order to be forgiven. In the name of Jesus. Amen.

THOUGHT FOR THE DAY: "I don't know why I feel this way," Richard said. "When he cut me, I shot him. I hit him in the leg, and he bled a lot. I wasn't even sorry, either. Now I wish I had gone ahead and killed him." We learn to hate people we have mistreated.

If you have robbed a man, you don't like him. If you have hurt someone, you don't like them. Jesus taught us we have to get rid of the hate in our hearts to live in God's spirit. We have to get rid of the hate and replace it with Christian love.

WEEK SEVEN: TO FORGIVE OTHERS

Day 5 ✷ Fellow Inmates

BIBLE VERSE: If you forgive others the wrongs they have done to you, your Father in heaven will also forgive you.

— Matthew 6:14

PRAYER: People have done me wrong, God. I think of some of them now. I think of people in here with me. My fellow inmates have lied to me, cursed me, and threatened me. They have stolen from me, wanted harm to come to me, and told lies about me. It is really hard to forgive them, Lord; yet I know Jesus Christ forgave those who mistreated him.

I am not just saying words, Lord. I really forgive them. I forgive them, Lord, so that I may obey your way of life. I forgive them in the name of Jesus. Amen.

THOUGHT FOR THE DAY: Two guys broke into my locker one night while I was asleep. They stole all my spending money—twelve dollars. The next day I found out who one of them was. A few days later I found out who the other one was. It took some prayer to forgive them, but I did. Mickey, a young inmate, said to me a few days later, "I learned how a Christian should act by watching you."

WEEK SEVEN: TO FORGIVE OTHERS

Day 6 ✸ Betrayers (Snitches)

BIBLE VERSE: Joseph's brothers . . . sent a message to Joseph: "Before our father died, he told us to ask you, 'Please forgive the crime your brothers committed when they wronged you.' Now please forgive us the wrong that we, the servants of your father's God, have done." Joseph cried when he received this message.

— Genesis 50:15-17

PRAYER: Of all people to forgive, God, snitches are the worst. Judas snitched on your son Jesus and had him arrested. Snitches are low and selfish, Lord. But you tell me to forgive them too. God, I am trying to do that. It is very hard to do. I need your grace and strength in order to forgive them.

In the name of Jesus I forget all thoughts of revenge. I will not hurt them although they have told bad things on me. In the name of Jesus I forgive those who have snitched on me. Amen.

THOUGHT FOR THE DAY: Joseph was one of God's people who went to prison. His own brothers sold him to strangers. They betrayed him. His own brothers! God spoke to Joseph and told him to forgive them. Joseph did so and received a blessing from the Lord. He came to be the real ruler of Egypt. God has a blessing for you as you forgive those who have betrayed you.

WEEK SEVEN: TO FORGIVE OTHERS

Day 7 ✵ Home-breakers

BIBLE VERSE: Do not judge others, and God will not judge you; do not condemn others, and God will not condemn you; forgive others, and God will forgive you.

— Luke 6:37

PRAYER: God, forgiving is so hard. And now comes the hardest part: to forgive someone who is breaking up my home. I am locked up and cannot earn money, cannot defend myself, cannot provide for my family. I must trust in you to do that, God.

With your Holy Spirit guiding me, and with Jesus in my heart, I am trying to forgive the one breaking up my home. But Lord, as I do this, I call on you to save my home. I forgive, and I trust in you. Amen.

THOUGHT FOR THE DAY: I sat on the steps of the prison. Beside me was a young man, Larry. He was sobbing as if he were breaking in two. Tears rolled down his cheeks. Between sobs, he said, "I'm losing my wife. I love my wife. I have two children. What is going on?"

Prisoners say, "Jody came." Jody is the "other guy," who moves in when you are in prison. Prison is one of the worst home-breakers in the world. One must be strong in the Lord to cope with "Jody." Let the Lord help you.

WEEK EIGHT: TO HAVE GOD'S FORGIVENESS

Day 1 ✻ Return to the Lord

BIBLE VERSE: Turn back to me, and I will turn to you.
— Malachi 3:7

PRAYER: Lord, I have gotten away from you. I have been far away living my own life. I have followed the evil ways of my own heart and not the ways of your heart. I have wasted my time, my money, my life.

I have gone away from you and I desire to come back to you, God. I return to you now—and you are returning to me! Praise the Lord! Amen.

THOUGHT FOR THE DAY: In the Gospel of Luke (15:11-32), a younger son left his home, his older brother, and his father. He went to a country far away and lived a life of sin. He woke up one morning missing his father and his home. He missed the good food and the joy of his home. He realized what a mess he had made of his life. He decided to return to his father. When he did, his father came running to meet him.

When we return to God, God comes to us!

WEEK EIGHT: TO HAVE GOD'S FORGIVENESS

Day 2 ✸ Ask God's Forgiveness

BIBLE VERSE: I will get up and go to my father and say, "Father, I have sinned against God and against you."

— Luke 15:18

PRAYER: O God, I confess to you my sin. I confess, God, not only that I have sinned, but that I am a sinner. Sin has been living in my heart.

I have not lived as I should. I have gone my own way instead of your way. I have let sin and selfishness live in my heart. Forgive me, O Lord, according to your mercy. In the name of Jesus. Amen.

THOUGHT FOR THE DAY: When we confess our sin to God, we are able to deal with it with God's help. We are ready for God to heal our sins and to purify our hearts.

In Luke 15, a son confessed his sin to his father. His father had already forgiven him and welcomed him back into his home. That is what happens to us when we confess to God. God forgives us and takes us back.

WEEK EIGHT: TO HAVE GOD'S FORGIVENESS

Day 3 ✷ Confess Your Sins

BIBLE VERSE: If we confess our sins to God, he will keep his promise and do what is right; he will forgive us our sins and purify us from all our wrongdoing.

— 1 John 1:9

PRAYER: God, I confess to you that I am a sinner. I confess specific sins of my life: [name them]. I bring my sins to you, O God. I recall your promise to forgive me and to cleanse me from wrongdoing. I claim your commitment to forgive and to cleanse. My sins are now forgiven, and I praise your name! Amen.

THOUGHT FOR THE DAY: What a verse! What a promise! God *never* goes back on his word. If you confess your sins, God *will* forgive your sins and cleanse you from *all* wrongdoing!

This verse brought me back to God after I had done wrong. I listed my sins and confessed them to the Lord. I knew that God had forgiven me. Praise God!

WEEK EIGHT: TO HAVE GOD'S FORGIVENESS

Day 4 ✷ Pray for Mercy

BIBLE VERSE: Be merciful to me, O God,
because of your constant love.
Because of your great mercy
wipe away my sins!
— Psalm 51:1

PRAYER: I have sinned. I have done wrong. I need you to forgive me, Lord. I cannot make up for what I have done. O God, have mercy on me! You have love, God. You are a God of kindness and love. Forgive me!

Take away my sins, O God, according to your tender mercies and your lovingkindness. Give me another chance at life, free from the burden of guilt caused by my sins. In the name of Jesus I pray. Amen.

THOUGHT FOR THE DAY: David wrote many of the Psalms. He wrote the one we read today. He was hurting very much. He was crying out to God. Alone with his thoughts, he remembered Uriah, the man he had had killed. He remembered Uriah's wife Bathsheba, whom he stole from Uriah. He knew he had strayed from God. He knew he couldn't make up for what he had done nor could he bring Uriah back to life. He asked God to have mercy on him. We too can pray for God's mercy.

WEEK EIGHT: TO HAVE GOD'S FORGIVENESS

Day 5 ✸ Turn from Sin

BIBLE VERSE: If they pray to me and repent and turn away from the evil they have been doing, then I will hear them in heaven, forgive their sins, and make their land prosperous again.

— 2 Chronicles 7:14

PRAYER: God, I seek to see your face and to know your ways. I turn from my bad ways. You say in your word that you will forgive our sin and heal us if we turn to you. I give up the ways of the world, O God, and turn to your ways! In the name of Jesus. Amen.

THOUGHT FOR THE DAY: Saul threatened Christians. He arrested them and threw them into prison. He supported the stoning of Stephen. He was on his way to Damascus to arrest the Christians there when suddenly he was changed. God changed Saul's heart, forgave him, changed his name to Paul, and began to use him (Acts 9:1-5).

Paul then preached the gospel, brought people to Jesus, and reached out to those who were hurting. Paul turned from his evil ways. God uses us when we truly turn from our evil ways.

WEEK EIGHT: TO HAVE GOD'S FORGIVENESS

Day 6 ✵ Pray for a Clean Heart

BIBLE VERSE: Create a pure heart in me, O God,
and put a new and loyal spirit in me.
— Psalm 51:10

PRAYER: I need a clean heart, O God. Only you can give me a clean and pure heart through your forgiveness. I so long for a new spirit within me. I need to live according to your laws and the laws of humanity.

I pray for a loyal spirit and a clean heart. Only you, God, can give me these. What a joy it will be to have a clean heart and a new, loyal spirit! In the name of Jesus. Amen.

THOUGHT FOR THE DAY: Are you burdened with guilt? Are you weighed down with a heart heavy from your sins and your actions? The Lord can give you a clean heart. And *only* the Lord can give you a clean heart!

God cleansed the heart of David by forgiving him and by giving him a new start in life with God's presence in him. God can do that for you too. God's spirit within you enables you to keep the laws of God *and* the laws of humanity.

Pray for a clean heart given by the Lord!

Day 7 ✸ Forgive Others

BIBLE VERSE: Our Father in heaven, . . . forgive us the wrongs we have done, as we forgive the wrongs that others have done to us.

— Matthew 6:12

PRAYER: You have taught me, Lord, that to be forgiven, I must be willing to forgive. It is hard to do that, God. So many people have hurt me. It is hard to forget what they have done. I cannot do it by myself, Lord. I need you to give me the grace to do it.

Yet I do forgive those who have done bad things to me, Lord. Jesus forgave all the people who had done wrong to him. In his name I forgive all who have done something to me. Amen.

THOUGHT FOR THE DAY: This Bible verse comes from a prayer that Jesus taught us to pray. God forgives your sins as you forgive those who sin against you.

Roy told me that his girlfriend's father opposed his loving her and writing to her. "He told her not to have anything else to do with me," Roy said. Roy was a Christian but had a hard feeling toward the man. "I really hate him," he said. Roy was praying that his girl would come back to him despite her father's prejudice. Roy had to forgive her father. He lost his girlfriend, but he gained peace in his soul through forgiveness.

WEEK NINE: TO KNOW THE WORD

Day 1 ✷ The Word Can Come to Me

BIBLE VERSE: O God, you are my God, and I long
for you.
My whole being desires you;
like a dry, worn-out, and waterless
land,
my soul is thirsty for you.
— Psalm 63:1

PRAYER: Lord, I am in need of your word! My soul pants for you, Lord. My heart hungers to know the word. My life is incomplete without knowing you. As your word went to others in prison, Lord, send it to me. Send it by preaching, or by song, or by a witness of yours. Lord, open your word to me that I may be filled with knowledge of you! In Jesus' name. Amen.

THOUGHT FOR THE DAY: I had been a preacher for thirty years. Yet as I was there in prison, I felt the need for the word of God in a stronger way than I had ever before felt. Then John came to see me. John is a young farmer who visits in the prison I was in. He opened the Bible and read the word to me. What a blessing! I literally wept as he did so. It was like rain on a hot, parched field!

The word of God will come to you. Someone will read the word to you in the name of Jesus! God will send the word to you!

WEEK NINE: TO KNOW THE WORD

Day 2 ✵ God Is the Word

BIBLE VERSE: In the beginning the Word already existed; the Word was with God, and the Word was God.

—John 1:1

PRAYER: God, I hunger and thirst to know the word! To know the word is to know you! Jesus knew the word. Jesus was and is the Word.

Lord, through the Bible I can come to know your word. Open my mind and my heart to the Bible, that I may know the word. Open the word to my heart that I may learn to walk in your ways, O God. Lead me through the Holy Spirit to know the word and to know you through the word! In the name of Jesus. Amen.

THOUGHT FOR THE DAY: Who is the word? What is the word? Jesus is the Word. Yet, we call the Bible the word. We come to know Jesus through God's book, the Bible. Yet the word is more. The word is truth. It is God made known to us!

The word has existed from the beginning and is made known to us through the Bible, as we are led by the Holy Spirit.

Getting to know the word is not hard. You don't have to be a preacher or be trained in theology. Just start reading the Bible and let God's spirit lead you to know the word.

…INE: TO KNOW THE WORD

Day 3 ✵ Jesus Is the Word

BIBLE VERSE: The Word became a human being and, full of grace and truth, lived among us. We saw his glory, the glory which he received as the Father's only Son.

—John 1:14

PRAYER: Lord Jesus, I am reaching for you. I'm afraid, yet I try not to be afraid. I don't know where you are leading me. I don't know where you are taking me. But Lord, I am following you day by day.

As I look for you, Jesus, I look through the Bible. For you are the Word made flesh! Lead me to know you better. Lead me to God's grace. In your name I pray. Amen.

THOUGHT FOR THE DAY: As I pick up the pen, I say and pray, "Lord Jesus, this is your pen, your hand, your paper. Write what you will, Lord."

"I am the Word," he says. "Come to me first, and I will lead you to the word. Take me by the hand and go with me. Don't worry about what you don't know." (*Amen*!) "Don't worry about what you can't read." (*Amen*!) "Just come and go with me. Don't be afraid." (*Read the word, and trust the Lord*!)

WEEK NINE: TO KNOW THE WORD

Day 4 ✷ We Live by the Word

BIBLE VERSE: Jesus answered, "The scripture says, 'Man cannot live on bread alone, but needs every word that God speaks.' "

— Matthew 4:4

PRAYER: God, I need your word! I need the spoken word and the written word. I need your word as my body needs food. I need your word as the desert needs water. O Lord, let me hear the gospel in preaching. Let me read and understand your word in the Bible. In the name of Jesus. Amen.

THOUGHT FOR THE DAY: There is the spoken word and the written word. We live by the word from God, which comes to us in both speaking and writing.

In prison, we had Bible studies and preaching every night. Why? Because in prison, as in life everywhere, a Christian lives by the word from God. A Christian receives the word from the Bible, from preaching, and from the witness of fellow Christians.

The word gives wisdom, strength, and guidance to our souls. Let us resolve in each prison cell to have a Bible study and prayer session each night. We live by the word of God!

WEEK NINE: TO KNOW THE WORD

Day 5 ✹ The Word Is Precious

BIBLE VERSE: Your commandments are my eternal
possession;
they are the joy of my heart.
— Psalm 119:111

PRAYER: O Lord, how I love your word! It is precious to me, God, but I have neglected it. I have failed to read it, failed to learn it, failed to let it speak to my heart. Forgive me!

I know that the word will lead me to you, Lord. I pray now for the will to read the word more often. I pray, Lord, that you will inspire me through the Holy Spirit to read the word each day! In Jesus' name. Amen.

THOUGHT FOR THE DAY: When I went to jail, I carried my Bible with me. My mother and father had given it to me when I was eight years old. I knew it could give me the hope and the strength I needed. Sometimes, after reading my Bible, I would just hold it. When I went to meals, I carried a small New Testament and read it while we waited in line.

The word is precious to me. It can be precious to you as well.

WEEK NINE: TO KNOW THE WORD

Day 6 ✷ The Word Protects Me

BIBLE VERSE: I keep your law in my heart,
so that I will not sin against you.
— Psalm 119:11

PRAYER: Keep me from sin, Lord. Fill my heart and my mind with your word so that I will not sin against you. Every time I have sinned, I have been weak in the word. Now I pray for your strength in the word so I may be kept free from sin. In the name of Jesus. Amen.

THOUGHT FOR THE DAY: Roy gave his heart to Jesus. He had carried a shank (a knife) in his socks. He laid down his shank and placed a New Testament in his shirt pocket. He traded in his shank for the Bible! Since that time he has read the word every day and has been living close to Jesus. Some people have laughed at him.

He has walked in the way of the Lord. As I saw him pull his New Testament from his shirt pocket, I remembered this verse, "I keep your law in my heart, so that I will not sin against you."

WEEK NINE: TO KNOW THE WORD

Day 7 ✷ Blessed Are Those Who Keep the Word

BIBLE VERSE: Jesus answered, "Rather, how happy are those who hear the word of God and obey it!"

— Luke 11:28

PRAYER: Lord, I don't need just to look at the Bible or to have it in my room. I need to read it, to hear it, to live it! I need to keep your word in my heart!

Many times, Lord, I have let a day go by when I did not read your word. Many times I did not hear the word when I could have. Many, many times I did not live and keep your word.

Give me a new start, Lord. Let the desire of the word burn in my heart like a fire! In Jesus' name. Amen.

THOUGHT FOR THE DAY: Do you want to make each day in prison rich and meaningful? Do you think this is impossible? It isn't when you have the word in your heart! You can have the fullness of Christ in your heart with the word.

Gary kept a New Testament in his pocket. When he went to a meal, he pulled it out and read it as he waited for his food or waited to put up his tray. Many others followed this example. He read the word and brought it with him when we had Bible study. He kept the word by living it!

WEEK TEN: TO LIVE THE WORD

Day 1 ✷ Do God's Will, Enter God's Kingdom

BIBLE VERSE: Not everyone who calls me "Lord, Lord" will enter the Kingdom of heaven, but only those who do what my Father in heaven wants them to do.

— Matthew 7:21

PRAYER: O Lord Jesus, you know it is hard to live the gospel, especially where I am. Yet you lived it where you were. Be my strength, Lord, to live the gospel today. I do not ask for tomorrow—just for today.

Let me love those around me today. Let me live the gospel by loving them no matter what they have done or said. Live through my life, Lord, today, that I may do your will. In your name I pray. Amen.

THOUGHT FOR THE DAY: Bud came to prayer meeting one night. He said it had been a long time since he had been a Christian. He got up and said, "Tonight I want to give my life back to God." But he never came back to prayer meeting. He never really changed. A week later he was caught selling dope. He *spoke* the faith but failed to *live* it. He failed to inherit the kingdom because he didn't live up to his words.

WEEK TEN: TO LIVE THE WORD

Day 2 ✷ Be Wise and Do His Word

BIBLE VERSE: Anyone who hears these words of mine and obeys them is like a wise man who built his house on rock.

— Matthew 7:24

PRAYER: Master builder, I am building my life even here in this place. Every day is a part of the building. Lord, I confess I have heard the word but failed to *live* the word. I have heard about love but have often practiced hate. I have heard about forgiveness but have practiced revenge.

Forgive me, Lord. Lead me to *do* your word as well as to *hear* your word. In the name of Jesus. Amen.

THOUGHT FOR THE DAY: Charles came to prayer meeting one night. He came back the next night and kept coming each night. One night he came forward to accept Jesus as his Savior. He professed Christ. He started reading the word. And he started *living* the word. He stopped cursing. He quit much of his arguing and became a witness to the power of Christ in his life.

Charles was a wise man. He started building on the foundation of *doing* God's word!

WEEK TEN: TO LIVE THE WORD

Day 3 ✵ Be Doers—Not Just Hearers

BIBLE VERSE: Do not deceive yourselves by just listening to his word; instead, put it into practice.

—James 1:22

PRAYER: Lord, I love to hear the gospel. It stirs my soul to hear your word. But Lord, I need to be a doer. I need to put the gospel into practice in my daily life.

Lord, I pray that the Holy Spirit comes into my heart and mind and inspires me to do the word. Make me live the word as well as hear it. Teach me to be true to myself and to you by living the gospel. Show me what to do next, Lord, in order to do the word. In the name of Jesus. Amen.

THOUGHT FOR THE DAY: Mickey and Tom got into an argument at prayer meeting in our camp. They were yelling and arguing over the way of baptism. I said to them, "Stop this! What kind of witness are you giving to those who do not believe?" Mickey then went to Tom and apologized.

Even in prison we can become "hearers only" of the gospel and fail to be doers of the word. To argue over theology has no place in prison. It turns off those who might want to become a Christian. To *live* the gospel is to be more concerned with putting it into practice.

WEEK TEN: TO LIVE THE WORD

Day 4 ✹ Inherit the Kingdom by Doing

BIBLE VERSE: Then the King will say to the people on his right, "Come, you that are blessed by my Father! Come and possess the kingdom which has been prepared for you ever since the creation of the world."

— Matthew 25:34

PRAYER: Lord God, many times right here in prison I have walked by my brothers or sisters in need of a helping hand. Right here, O Lord, I have thought of myself more than of others.

Forgive me, God! In the name of Jesus, give me eyes to see the needs of others, give me hands to help them carry their loads. Let me be a servant of yours, Lord, in this place. In the name of Jesus. Amen.

THOUGHT FOR THE DAY: When Jesus made the statement in the Bible verse above, he was talking about visiting prisoners, feeding hungry people, caring for the sick, and doing ministry to people in need. To do these things is, indeed, to *live* God's word.

You can be God's person where you are! Be a friend to someone in need. Offer a prayer for a brother or sister. Be God's witness where you are and live the word!

Week Ten: To Live the Word

Day 5 ✵ Obey God's Commandments

Bible Verse: Happy are those who wash their robes clean and so have the right to eat the fruit from the tree of life and to go through the gates into the city.

— Revelation 22:14

Prayer: Lord God, when I get up in the morning, my heart is too weak to do your will. I look at where I am, how long I've been here, and how long I must stay. I feel too weak to follow you, and sometimes I ask, "Why?" Then I go about the day, forgetting about you and your plan for my life. I pray, Lord, for the Holy Spirit to quicken my heart to do your will. In the name of Jesus. Amen.

Thought for the Day: A central message in the Bible is to do and to live the word of God. God's word is God's will for your life. *Do God's word!*

I have failed to do this so many times. When I do God's word, I notice how different my actions are compared with the actions of many people around me. Jesus has dared us to be different—to take our cue in life from God's word and God's will rather than from the actions of those around us.

WEEK TEN: TO LIVE THE WORD

Day 6 ✷ Do Things Pleasing to God

BIBLE VERSE: We receive from him whatever we ask, because we obey his commands and do what pleases him.

—1 John 3:22

PRAYER: O God, I want to be pleasing to you and to do your will in my life. I don't know how to do this. So far my life has not been pleasing to you because I have lived it my way rather than your way.

Forgive me, Lord, when I do things that are against your will. I repent of these actions anew, and give myself to doing your will. In Jesus' name. Amen.

THOUGHT FOR THE DAY: One-Eye, a new inmate with a glass eye, stood up at prayer meeting. We had just finished singing a song. One-Eye said, "I'll sing one." "Fine," I responded. "Come on." He came up front, cocked his head to one side, and sang a beautiful song. He had written the song himself. It was a witness to the Lord. He had pleased God by giving witness to God in the way that he could.

When we do things pleasing to God and keep God's commandments, we are *doing* God's word—not just hearing it.

WEEK TEN: TO LIVE THE WORD

Day 7 ✻ A Person of God Does Good

BIBLE VERSE: My dear friend, do not imitate what is bad, but imitate what is good. Whoever does good belongs to God; whoever does what is bad has not seen God.

— 3 John 11

PRAYER: God, we thank you for the example of faith that you gave us in Jesus Christ. He showed us what it is like to have faith. God, you taught us how to live our faith by becoming one of us and doing it yourself!

Lord, in the name of Jesus I pray that you will teach me how to live out my faith day by day! Grant, Lord, that I may *live* the word every day, right here where I am! I pray in Jesus' name. Amen.

THOUGHT FOR THE DAY: Our problem is *not* that we don't know what is right. Our problem is that we fail to *do* what we know is right!

Act on your faith! Practice the love of God! An older prisoner didn't have a towel. He asked me if I could get him one. At first I was irritated to be bothered. Then I asked myself, *What would Jesus do?* I gave him my only towel. He smiled and said, "Thank you." The next morning someone else gave me a towel.

WEEK ELEVEN: TO LIVE IN CHRIST

Day 1 ✷ Remain United to Christ

BIBLE VERSE: Remain united to me, and I will remain united to you. A branch cannot bear fruit by itself; it can do so only if it remains in the vine. In the same way you cannot bear fruit unless you remain in me.

— John 15:4

PRAYER: Lord Jesus, to live according to God's will is my goal. I long to remain united to you, to live in you, so that I can live by God's will. My life needs to serve God's purpose. Only by living in you, Lord, can I do this.

I give myself to you anew, Lord, to remain united to you. I give myself to you, to live according to God's will. In your name. Amen.

THOUGHT FOR THE DAY: All of life has a purpose. The pecan tree bears pecans. A cow provides milk and meat. Your life has purpose in God. Your purpose is to bear fruit for Christ—witnessing to others about Christ's love and inviting them to meet Jesus and accept salvation.

How do you do this? You serve your purpose by living in Christ, by remaining united to Christ. You don't do it just by prayer or just by worship—but by living each day, a day at a time, according to God's will!

Week Eleven: To Live in Christ

Day 2 ✵ Keep God's Commandments

Bible Verse: If you love me, you will obey my commandments.

—John 14:15

Prayer: Lord, down deep I desire to keep your commandments, your laws. When I fail to do this, I feel guilty and unworthy. But it is so hard, Lord. I pray for daily strength from you.

Lord, I pray that today I will live according to your will. I do love you, Lord, with all of my heart and soul! In the name of Jesus I pray. Amen.

Thought for the Day: Jesus said if we are to love him, we will keep his commandments. How true! We cannot love Jesus and ignore how he taught us to live. If we truly love Jesus more than the things of this world, we will keep his commandments.

What were the commandments Jesus taught us? To love God and to love others as ourselves. If we do this, we will be walking in God's way.

WEEK ELEVEN: TO LIVE IN CHRIST

Day 3 ✷ Have the Mind of Christ

BIBLE VERSE: The attitude you should have is the one that Christ Jesus had.

— Philippians 2:5

PRAYER: O Lord Jesus, I seek your mind to be in me. I seek to think as you would think, Lord, to act as you would act. I seek a new mind in the Lord! Empty my old mind of the thoughts and habits of sin, and fill my mind with your true holiness. Fill my mind with your thoughts and ways that I may think and act more like you. Fill my life with your presence, Lord. In your name. Amen.

THOUGHT FOR THE DAY: Your mind is the most important part of your whole being. Your mind decides the way you act. Every action is based on a decision. If you curse, you have *decided* to curse. Then cursing becomes a habit. If you take drugs, you have *decided* to take drugs. If you do not take drugs, you have *decided* that also. If you praise God, you have *decided* to praise God. Then praise becomes a habit!

Let Christ's mind be in you. When the mind of Christ is in you, you have total victory.

WEEK ELEVEN: TO LIVE IN CHRIST

Day 4 ✻ Renew Your Mind in Christ

BIBLE VERSE: Do not conform yourselves to the standards of this world, but let God transform you inwardly by a complete change of your mind. Then you will be able to know the will of God—what is good and is pleasing to him and is perfect.

— Romans 12:2

PRAYER: God, I give my mind to you. I offer you my thoughts, my life, but above all my mind. My mind is the most important part of me. I give my mind to you, God. I pray for the renewal of my mind through Christ Jesus, my Lord! In the name of Jesus. Amen.

THOUGHT FOR THE DAY: A thermometer indicates the rise and fall of a room's temperature. A thermostat controls the temperature of the room. The word of God calls you to be a thermostat, not a thermometer. That is, as Christians we are to control our environment for the Lord—not to be controlled by it.

As a Christian, we are not to be conformed to this world. If others curse, you don't have to. If others lie, you don't have to. By renewing your mind in Christ, you can transform part of your world for God.

WEEK ELEVEN: TO LIVE IN CHRIST

Day 5 ✷ Let Christ Live in You

BIBLE VERSE: It is no longer I who live, but it is Christ who lives in me. This life that I live now, I live by faith in the Son of God, who loved me and gave his life for me.

— Galatians 2:20

PRAYER: Lord Christ, I give myself to you. I place my life in your hands. I commit myself to you, Lord!

Live in me this day. Live *through* me this day. Here in prison, Lord, let your light shine through my life. Live in me, Lord! In your name. Amen.

THOUGHT FOR THE DAY: The late Dr. Martin Luther King, Jr., wrote, "So I say to you, seek God and discover Him and make Him a power in your life. Without Him all of our efforts turn to ashes and our sunrises into darkest nights. Without Him, life is a meaningless drama with the decisive scenes missing. But with Him we are able to rise from the fatigue of despair to the buoyancy of hope. With Him we are able to rise from the midnight of desperation to the daybreak of joy."[2]

Dr. King, who, like us, had spent nights of desperation in jail, found in Christ the daybreak of joy! You can too by letting Christ live in your heart!

---

[2]Martin Luther King, Jr., *The Words of Martin Luther King, Jr.* (New York: Newmarket Press, 1983), p. 64.

Week Eleven: To Live in Christ

Day 6 ✷ You Can Live in Christ

Bible Verse: My Father's glory is shown by your bearing much fruit; and in this way you become my disciples. I love you just as the Father loves me; remain in my love.

— John 15:8-9

Prayer: Christ Jesus, I know I can live in you and you in me. Every day can be a day for you. You need people to live for you, Lord—wherever they are. I want to be your person while I am here in prison. I want to show glory to you by being your witness and bearing fruit for you.

I praise you, Christ Jesus, and in your name I pray. Amen.

Thought for the Day: It's one thing to talk about Christ. It's another to live *in* Christ and to let Christ live *in* you. You *can* live in Christ. Everyone can! A person in prison can live in Christ!

Mickey is a young inmate with a wife and two children. He is serving four years for burglary. Mickey lives in Christ every day. He studies the word. He prays. He smiles. He lives in Christ day by day. You can too!

Week Eleven: To Live in Christ

Day 7 ✷ Trust God for the Future

Bible Verse: He will wipe away all tears from their eyes. There will be no more death, no more grief or crying or pain. The old things have disappeared.

— Revelation 21:4

Prayer: God, when I think about the future, I get worried. Yet you have told me not to worry about the future, but to trust in you!

I do that now, Lord. I trust in you—not in myself—for my future. God, I pray that today will be a day full of trust. Take away my worry and give me trust in you. In the name of Jesus. Amen.

Thought for the Day: Living in Christ applies to the future as well as the present. No more tears! No more death! No more grief or crying or pain!

How do you live in Christ for the future? You trust God! Don't worry about tomorrow! Trust it to God. God's future is better than your future! God can plan for you better than you can plan for yourself.

WEEK TWELVE: FOR GROWTH IN CHRIST

Day 1 ✷ Study the Word

BIBLE VERSE: Do your best to win full approval in God's sight, as a worker who is not ashamed of his work, one who correctly teaches the message of God's truth.

— 2 Timothy 2:15

PRAYER: I rejoice in your word, O God! Your word is truth and life. I do not know your word as I should. I do not know your word as well as I hope to.

God, I don't read or understand that well. I just pray for the Holy Spirit to guide me to understand your word as I am able. Teach me through your Holy Spirit to study your word and to learn it. In Jesus' name. Amen.

THOUGHT FOR THE DAY: God's word has the answer to your problems, the answer to your life, and untold riches in heaven for you. It is the greatest resource for living in the entire world. God's word can take the hell out of prison life and put some heaven into it! God's word can make it possible for you to live a day at a time in victory. When applied to your life, God's word could even bring a quicker release for you from prison—because the word helps you get along with others much better. Study the word!

WEEK TWELVE: FOR GROWTH IN CHRIST

Day 2 ✷ Understand the Word

BIBLE VERSE: While I was still in prison in the courtyard, the LORD's message came to me again. The LORD, who made the earth, who formed it and set it in place, spoke to me. He whose name is the LORD said, "Call to me, and I will answer you; I will tell you wonderful and marvelous things that you know nothing about."

— Jeremiah 33:1-3

PRAYER: Your word comes to me, Lord. It will not be denied. Open my mind and my heart that I may receive it. Make it known to me! While I am in prison, Lord, as Jeremiah was in prison, may your word come in fullness and as strength to me. Teach me of "wonderful and marvelous things" that I know nothing about! In the name of Jesus. Amen.

THOUGHT FOR THE DAY: Jeremiah, the man of God, was shut up in prison. Yet the word of the Lord came to him there! The word of the Lord comes to folks in prison today. Christians visit. Inmates read the word. People pray for prisoners, pray for *you*.

I was giving out Bibles one night. A young inmate said, "I don't read very well." I said, "Then hold it in your hands." I prayed for him and helped him read it, and I read it to him. The word came to him too!

WEEK TWELVE: FOR GROWTH IN CHRIST

Day 3 ✷ Pray Each Day

BIBLE VERSE: Pray at all times.

— 1 Thessalonians 5:17

PRAYER: Teach me to pray, O Lord. Lead me to learn how to pray when things go well. Lead me to pray when things go wrong. Set my mind to pray at all times, O Lord.

I have often forgotten to pray. I quit praying for awhile. Now I want to get back to praying all the time. Turn me to you, O Lord, when I fail to pray. In the name of Jesus. Amen.

THOUGHT FOR THE DAY: Dal was a middle-aged man in prison. He loved the Lord. One morning he came rushing over to me weeping. "What is wrong?" I asked. "My best friend got killed in a wreck," he sobbed. To make matters worse, Dal could not go to the funeral because he was in prison. "Let's pray," I said. I put my arm on his shoulder, and we prayed.

To pray at all times is to pray on all occasions—good and bad, happy and sad.

WEEK TWELVE: FOR GROWTH IN CHRIST

Day 4 ✹ Pray When Things Go Wrong

BIBLE VERSE: About midnight Paul and Silas were praying and singing hymns to God, and the other prisoners were listening to them.

— Acts 16:25

PRAYER: I am in jail. I am sad, Jesus, and I am separated from people who love me. I am surrounded by people who could care less what happens to me. Some even hate me.

Teach me not to back away from you when things are going wrong, but to draw nearer to you. Thank you for your spirit within me. Thank you, Jesus, for your love for me. Thank you for all you are and all you do. Thank you, Jesus, for all your blessings! In your name I pray. Amen.

THOUGHT FOR THE DAY: Paul and Silas were in jail. It was midnight. Things were as bad as they could be. Yet they prayed to God and sang hymns.

Our prayers when things are going bad need to consist of praise as well as pleas for help. What could be worse than midnight in jail? You can't sleep. You are lonely, lying there thinking about home and the persons you love. Try praying. Try praising God at midnight. When things are at their worst, pray and praise!

WEEK TWELVE: FOR GROWTH IN CHRIST

Day 5 ✷ Receive the Holy Spirit

BIBLE VERSE: I will ask the Father, and he will give you another Helper, who will stay with you forever. He is the Spirit, who reveals the truth about God. The world cannot receive him, because it cannot see him or know him. But you know him, because he remains with you and is in you.

—John 14:16-17

PRAYER: O Lord, fill my empty life with your Holy Spirit. Like a locust shell, I am dead and hollow without you. I need the Holy Spirit, Lord. I need the Spirit to reveal the truth to me. I pray now for the coming of your Holy Spirit more fully into my life. Fill me now, Lord, with the Spirit. In the name of Jesus. Amen.

THOUGHT FOR THE DAY: When I was a boy, I found empty locust shells on trees. I picked them off and looked at them. Later I learned that the locust had popped out of the shell and flown away.

If we are without the Holy Spirit, our lives are like empty locust shells. But God gives us the Holy Spirit, and the Spirit fills our lives with God's love and power.

Day 6 ✷ Pray in the Spirit

BIBLE VERSE: And God, who sees into our hearts, knows what the thought of the Spirit is; because the Spirit pleads with God on behalf of his people and in accordance with his will.

— Romans 8:27

PRAYER: How do I come to you, O God? What do I say? I don't know. But you know, Lord. You know what I should pray for. You know what I really need. I only know what I *think* I need. Your Spirit intercedes for me to bring your will to my life and to fill my deepest needs. Lord, I pray in your Holy Spirit now and ask you to fill my real needs. I ask for the intercession of your Holy Spirit. In Jesus' name. Amen.

THOUGHT FOR THE DAY: The Holy Spirit strengthens our prayer life in the Lord. The Spirit even prays *for* us when we don't know what to pray. This means the Spirit even prays for persons and for situations that we don't know we need to pray for.

As we allow the Holy Spirit to fill us as we pray, the Spirit is praying for us and for others as the Spirit knows and understands the need.

WEEK TWELVE: FOR GROWTH IN CHRIST

Day 7 ✵ Witness for Jesus

BIBLE VERSE: Are they Christ's servants? I sound like a madman—but I am a better servant than they are! I have worked much harder, I have been in prison more times, I have been whipped much more, and I have been near death more often.

— 2 Corinthians 11:23

PRAYER: Use my life, O Lord. My tongue shall be your tongue. My words shall be your words. I desire to speak your word of life to those around me. I seek to bring your word of life to your people in prison. Teach me to speak your words—words of witness, praise, hope, and love. In the name of Jesus, I give my words to you! Amen.

THOUGHT FOR THE DAY: Saul was cruel in his pursuit and persecution of Christians—before *he* gave *his heart* to Christ. He hunted Christians like animals. He threw them in jail and had them killed.

But when he saw the light of Christ, Saul completely changed—even his name was new, "Paul." He stopped putting people in jail. Instead he was put in jail himself, for Christ. The hunter became the hunted, but for Christ. Jesus took a cruel, relentless man and turned his life into one of the greatest powers for God the world has ever seen.

Christ can do that for you!

WEEK THIRTEEN: FOR SELF-CONTROL

Day 1 ✱ Depression

BIBLE VERSE: "Do not be worried and upset," Jesus told them. "Believe in God and believe also in me."

—John 14:1

PRAYER: At times I feel very low, God. This place and these people are more than I can take sometimes. I don't feel like I can hold out much longer.

I do believe in you, God. I do believe in the Lord Jesus. Take away my sadness and give me the joy of the Lord in my life. Guide me to believe ever more strongly in you, Lord, and in your Son Jesus Christ. In the name of Jesus I pray. Amen.

THOUGHT FOR THE DAY: It is believed that Abraham Lincoln said, "Every person is as happy as he makes up his mind to be." You do have control over depression in your life! That is the reason Jesus said, "Do not be worried and upset."

He told us how to control depression. Control it with faith in God and faith in Jesus Christ. Believe in God! Believe in Jesus Christ! This will help drive away depression.

WEEK THIRTEEN: FOR SELF-CONTROL

Day 2 ✷ Anger

BIBLE VERSE: If you stay calm, you are wise, but if you have a hot temper, you only show how stupid you are.
— Proverbs 14:29

PRAYER: Lord, I pray for your spirit to control my mind, my emotions, and especially my anger. When I am angry at those around me, I get into trouble, Lord. A single minute or second in anger can cost me many years of trouble. Put a bridle on my temper, Lord, to hold it in. When I get mad, teach me to walk away and to pray instead of "going off" on someone. I know that I am at a disadvantage. Officers and others can mistreat me, but I must not respond. That is hard to learn, God. Teach me to hold my temper. In the name of Jesus. Amen.

THOUGHT FOR THE DAY: Randy had a hot temper. One day an officer corrected him. Randy "went off" in a fit of rage. The officer had him handcuffed and taken to a security unit. Randy's fit of temper cost him dearly.

Prison is a place where one has to subject one's mind and will to abuse and not strike back. That is hard to do. Be stronger than those who would abuse you. Take it, and go on. Be slow to anger.

WEEK THIRTEEN: FOR SELF-CONTROL

Day 3 ✷ Resentment

BIBLE VERSE: Guard against turning back from the grace of God. Let no one become like a bitter plant that grows up and causes many troubles with its poison.

— Hebrews 12:15

PRAYER: Put out the fire of anger in me, O God. Pour the waters of your love into my heart that I may learn to love my enemies and bless those who curse me. You know this is hard, Lord. Your son blessed and forgave those who put him on the cross.

I yearn to love you. I yearn to love others as your children, God. I do not wish to hurt them or you. Take away my anger and resentment. Put me under your control. In the name of Jesus. Amen.

THOUGHT FOR THE DAY: James got into moods. Sometimes he would speak to people. Sometimes he wouldn't. The cause of his moods was resentment. A slow fire of resentment and anger burned inside him. He was like a mattress that caught on fire from a lit cigarette. It just smoldered, burning slowly until it leaped into flames. Resentment is a slow fire burning within us. It will consume and destroy us and those around us until it is put out with the water of God's love. Don't be destroyed by resentment. Let God's love come into your life.

WEEK THIRTEEN: FOR SELF-CONTROL

Day 4 ✷ Griping

BIBLE VERSE: Jesus answered, "Stop grumbling among yourselves."

—John 6:43

PRAYER: Thank you, God, for bread to eat. Many people have none. Thank you, God, for a bed to sleep on, no matter how hard it is. Millions of your children have nothing but the ground or a street to sleep on. Thank you, God, for salvation. Thank you for the word!

Forgive me, Lord, for griping. Forgive me for taking you for granted. Give me your joy in my heart! In the name of Jesus. Amen.

THOUGHT FOR THE DAY: Griping is a way of life in prison. Almost everybody gripes—inmates, guards, officials. Nowhere is there more griping or tearing others down than in prisons and jails. Griping is negative thought and negative words. Griping hurts you and everyone around you.

Stop your griping! Start praising God! Paul and Silas praised God in jail. They did not gripe or complain. Give God a chance in your life and in your jail by praising him instead of griping!

WEEK THIRTEEN: FOR SELF-CONTROL

Day 5 ✵ Criticism

BIBLE VERSE: Do not judge others, so that God will not judge you, for God will judge you in the same way you judge others, and he will apply to you the same rules you apply to others.

— Matthew 7:1-2

PRAYER: Every single person is your child, O Lord—every single person. I have as many sins and faults as anyone else. When I criticize others, I only make a mess of things. I know I would get along better if I quit saying bad things about others and started finding good in them. Teach me, O Lord, to break the habit of finding fault in others and to start the habit of looking for the good in them. In the name of Jesus. Amen.

THOUGHT FOR THE DAY: Living in prison is like living in a zoo. You are on display to others around you all the time. Every spot and blemish is visible. You can see faults in others, and others can see them in you. It is so easy to criticize others. "John is a liar." "Joe can't be trusted." "Robert is a no-good. . . ." On it goes.

Stop it! Stop criticizing others! It has to stop somewhere. Let it stop with you for Jesus' sake. Find the good in others and let them know it!

WEEK THIRTEEN: FOR SELF-CONTROL

Day 6 ✷ Boredom

BIBLE VERSE: They said to each other, "Wasn't it like a fire burning in us when he [Jesus] talked to us on the road and explained the Scriptures to us?"

— Luke 24:32

PRAYER: Time is so important, Lord. Every minute is a chance to grow and to do your will. I don't need to waste time here or to throw it away. I need to use my time to get excited about your word! Open the word to my heart and mind, Lord. Make my heart burn with excitement within me as I learn and grow in your word! In the name of Jesus. Amen.

THOUGHT FOR THE DAY: Prison has to be one of the most boring places on earth. Part of the punishment of prison life is the forced, grinding pace of unused hours and days. One sees the same walls, hears the same voices, watches the same faces, eats the same kind of food—day after day. How boring! How tedious and tasteless the hours!

But how wonderful it is to be excited! How does one become excited in prison—the Capital of Boredom? Through the word of God! The word is the most exciting thing in the world. And you can get excited over the word right here in prison!

WEEK THIRTEEN: FOR SELF-CONTROL

Day 7 ✷ Gambling

BIBLE VERSE: It is better to have a little, honestly earned, than to have a large income, dishonestly gained.
— Proverbs 16:8

PRAYER: I am tempted, Lord Jesus, to gamble here. I am not working for income. I have time on my hands. It seems an easy way to get something for nothing. Teach me, Lord, to know when I am tempted to gamble.

Lord Jesus, you resisted the temptation to "get something for nothing." When you were hungry and Satan tempted you to turn stone into bread, you set the example for me and for others by saying no (Luke 4:1-4). Make me say no to gambling. In your name. Amen.

THOUGHT FOR THE DAY: Gambling leads to other sins. Leroy stole a radio. Jimmy had been gambling and lost some money. He stole the radio from Leroy after he lost the money. Leroy got angry and stole a radio from Charles. Leroy got locked down. Jimmy got into trouble too.

Gambling only puts money into the hands of those "smarter" and more crooked than you. They wouldn't be gambling with you if the chances were "even." Don't be dumb. Be smart. Say no when you are tempted to gamble.

WEEK FOURTEEN: FOR VICTORY OVER SELF

Day 1 ✷ Drinking Alcohol

BIBLE VERSE: Do not get drunk with wine, which will only ruin you; instead, be filled with the Spirit.

— Ephesians 5:18

PRAYER: Lord, I need victory over my drinking. I really need to quit. I pray for your spirit to conquer my desire to drink alcohol. It has gotten me into much trouble. Take away my need and desire for it, Lord.

Give me a clear mind and heart, free from the need to drink. Take away the craving from my mind and body. Bring me victory, Lord, over alcohol! In the name of Jesus. Amen.

THOUGHT FOR THE DAY: William talked with me. He has been in jail three times. He is married and has three children. He said, "My problem is drinking." He would get drunk any time he could. Even in jail he managed to get alcohol and get drunk. I said, "Until you get victory over that, you will stay in trouble."

Jesus Christ can and does deliver people from alcohol. He can and will deliver you if you call on him!

WEEK FOURTEEN: FOR VICTORY OVER SELF

Day 2 ✷ Taking Drugs

BIBLE VERSE: I have the strength to face all conditions by the power that Christ gives me.

— Philippians 4:13

PRAYER: I am tired of needing drugs, God. I have been a slave to the habit, to my craving for drugs. I need to be free, God! You teach in your word that I can do all things through the power of Christ.

I give my life to you, God. I give you my body, my mind, my spirit. I call on you to deliver me from the slavery of drugs. Through the power of Christ, set me free from drugs. I know I can do all things through Christ, who gives me strength! In the name of Jesus. Amen.

THOUGHT FOR THE DAY: Can Christ really bring victory over drugs? *Yes.* Can Christ do that while a person is in prison? *Yes.*

Roy is twenty-eight years old. He was on marijuana, cocaine, heroin, and, according to him, anything he could get. He ran con games and did armed robbery to get drugs. But then he found Jesus Christ! Roy gave his life to Jesus. Now Roy does no drugs at all. He lives and witnesses for Jesus.

Jesus Christ can conquer drugs in your life! Praise Christ!

Week Fourteen: For Victory over Self

Day 3 ✱ Smoking Cigarettes

Bible Verse: But thanks be to God who gives us the victory through our Lord Jesus Christ!

— 1 Corinthians 15:57

Prayer: I do things, Lord, I don't want to do. I do them because I can't seem to stop. I smoke because I can't seem to stop. It costs me money. It hurts my health.

God, in the name of Jesus, I claim victory over smoking. I lay down my cigarettes, and I give them to you. You have given me the victory through the power of Christ! In the name of Jesus. Amen.

Thought for the Day: Roy was leading our prayer meeting one night. He said, "The Lord can help you give up smoking. The Lord wants you to quit smoking!" The next morning Billy went to Roy and said, "I prayed last night. The Lord told me to quit smoking." Billy quit. "I feel 100 percent better," he said.

You can quit smoking too! You don't have to wait until you get out of prison to quit smoking. You can quit right now. Jesus Christ can help you win victory over cigarettes!

WEEK FOURTEEN: FOR VICTORY OVER SELF

Day 4 ✵ Lust

BIBLE VERSE: You have heard that it was said, "Do not commit adultery." But now I tell you: anyone who looks at a woman and wants to possess her is guilty of committing adultery with her in his heart.

— Matthew 5:27-28

PRAYER: Only you, God, know how I long for the physical love of another person. Here I am locked up, Lord. Against my basic nature, I am denied access to those of the opposite sex.

Lord, give me strength, in this unnatural situation, to cope with it with victory. Give me your power to channel the desires of my body and heart into creative living for you. In the name of Jesus. Amen.

THOUGHT FOR THE DAY: Prison is a testing place. The confinement it places on one—whether male or female—is especially hard. Men and women who are denied normal social interchange with those of the opposite sex often develop an abnormal sense of desire.

What are we to do with our sexual desires when we are locked up? Give them to Jesus! The Lord knows and understands. Christ can take lust from one's heart and turn it into creative activity.

WEEK FOURTEEN: FOR VICTORY OVER SELF

Day 5 ✷ Profanity

BIBLE VERSE: You can be sure that on the Judgment Day you will have to give account of every useless word you have ever spoken. Your words will be used to judge you—to declare you either innocent or guilty.

— Matthew 12: 36-37

PRAYER: By my words, Lord, I am judged. By my words I affect my own destiny and that of others around me. I know how important my words are to me and to you, Lord.

I have cursed. I have used your name in vain. I ask you to forgive me. I give my words to you, God. Amen.

THOUGHT FOR THE DAY: Al said, "Something happened to my speech the last six years I have been in prison. I cuss all the time. I use God's name in vain. My speech has gotten terrible." That happens if we allow it. Al continued, "God don't like that." Al was right. The Lord does hear what we say. Cursing comes from a heart that is out of fellowship with God.

Be strong in the Lord. Lay down your cursing. Clean up your speech. See how God will bless you!

WEEK FOURTEEN: FOR VICTORY OVER SELF

Day 6 ✷ Lying

BIBLE VERSE: There are seven things that the LORD hates and cannot tolerate:
A proud look,
a lying tongue,
hands that kill innocent people,
a mind that thinks up wicked plans,
feet that hurry off to do evil,
a witness who tells one lie after another,
and someone who stirs up trouble
among friends.

— Proverbs 6:16-19

PRAYER: I know you don't like me to lie. But Lord, it seems to me that when I tell the truth, I just get into more trouble. If I tell what I know on other people, they'll get hurt and I'll be a snitch. The prisoners will hurt me. Please help me, Lord, to live in the truth even though it might get me into trouble around here. I trust you, Lord. Amen.

THOUGHT FOR THE DAY: Telling the truth can get you into trouble, either with the law or with the other people in prison. But in the long run telling the truth saves you from more trouble than it causes you. God stays with you when you tell the truth. It's far better to have God with you when you live the truth than to have others with you when you don't. Speak and live the truth.

WEEK FOURTEEN: FOR VICTORY OVER SELF

Day 7 ✷ Stealing

BIBLE VERSE: If you used to rob, you must stop robbing and start working, in order to earn an honest living for yourself and to be able to help the poor.

— Ephesians 4:28

PRAYER: Lord, you know the needs of my life and that of my loved ones. You know that we do not live by bread alone. I have taken from others that which belonged to them. I ask you to forgive me, Lord. I turn now from any form of stealing or dishonesty. I turn to you, Lord, for my needs. In the name of Jesus. Amen.

THOUGHT FOR THE DAY: Stealing, like lying, is a habit. It is a habit of sin. Whether it is a pencil or the pencil factory, stealing is a violation of the law of God.

Zaccheus cheated people out of their money. When he came to Jesus, he realized his wrong act and repented. He turned from his dishonest ways. Jesus said salvation had come to Zaccheus' house that day (Luke 19:1-10).

God forgives us as we repent and turn from any dishonest ways of our lives. Trust God to help provide your needs, and work when and as you can to honestly get what you need. God does provide.

WEEK FIFTEEN: FOR HEALING

Day 1 ✷ Jesus Can Heal

BIBLE VERSE: Once Jesus was in a town where there was a man who was suffering from a dreaded skin disease. When he saw Jesus, he threw himself down and begged him, "Sir, if you want to, you can make me clean!" Jesus reached out and touched him. "I do want to," he answered. "Be clean!" At once the disease left the man.

— Luke 5:12-13

PRAYER: Lord Jesus, we know that you can heal. You are the Great Healer. You healed when you were here on this earth, and you heal today. You can heal my body, my mind, my spirit. You cast out demons. You heal diseases.

Prison is no place to be sick, Lord. I pray now for my healing. Heal my spirit of low feelings. Heal my body of its disease. In your name. Amen.

THOUGHT FOR THE DAY: Someone asked me, "Do you believe in faith healing?" I said, "No, but I believe in God's healing." God heals with the help and cooperation of doctors, medicine, and all of the tools of healing we have, along with the power of faith!

It is easy to get sick in prison. You don't get enough sleep and rest. You eat food that has little nutrition. You suffer from lack of exercise and a constant bombardment of noise and irritation. You need the healing power of Jesus in prison!

WEEK FIFTEEN: FOR HEALING

Day 2 ✷ Jesus Casts Out Demons

BIBLE VERSE: Jesus healed many who were sick with all kinds of diseases and drove out many demons. He would not let the demons say anything, because they knew who he was.

— Mark 1:34

PRAYER: Lord God, you can heal. My body is your temple. You want me to be well. You want all of your children to be well. I ask you in the name of Jesus to give me a mind whole in the Lord! Free me from depression, from self-pity, from worry. Make me well from any disease. Free me from sickness of body and spirit so that I may serve you fully. In the name of Jesus. Amen.

THOUGHT FOR THE DAY: The healing Jesus did was without regard to race, money, or male or female. He healed many people with all kinds of disorders!

Big Dave was feeling so low he could hardly get up out of bed. Our prayer group met by his bunk one night. We prayed earnestly for Dave. We did not know why he was feeling so low, but we called on Christ to help him. After awhile, Big Dave got up and started walking. Then he smiled and said, "I feel like I'm lifted!" We praised God!

Try calling on God. God loves you and will help you!

WEEK FIFTEEN: FOR HEALING

Day 3 ✷ Jesus Heals the Broken-hearted

BIBLE VERSE: It is good to sing praise to our God;
it is pleasant and right to praise
him . . .
He heals the broken-hearted and
bandages their wounds.
— Psalm 147:1, 3

PRAYER: You really do heal broken hearts, Lord. You know my heart is broken. It is broken because I have to be here. It is broken because I am separated from those who love me. It is broken because I am no longer respected. My heart is broken, Lord. But you heal the broken-hearted.

Heal and bandage me, O Lord. Bring me peace of mind, heart, and soul. In your name. Amen.

THOUGHT FOR THE DAY: Robert's wife divorced him while he was in prison. It broke his heart. It made him bitter and angry. But Robert found the Lord in his situation. The Lord healed his broken heart and gave him peace and faith to face the future. Jesus heals our broken hearts as well as our broken bodies. Praise the Lord!

WEEK FIFTEEN: FOR HEALING

Day 4 ✸ Jesus Laid on Hands, Healed

BIBLE VERSE: After sunset all who had friends who were sick with various diseases brought them to Jesus; he placed his hands on every one of them and healed them all.

— Luke 4:40

PRAYER: Lord of all people, Lord of health and life, I turn to you now. May the hand of a believer rest on me to bring healing to my mind and my body. You laid hands on God's children for healing. You taught your followers to lay on hands for healing. I do not understand all about it, Lord. I simply trust in you. In your name. Amen.

THOUGHT FOR THE DAY: Clyde had been in solitary lockdown. He was crying and yelling when he got out of solitary. I asked him, "Clyde, what's wrong? Why are you so upset?"

He replied, "I have a terrible headache. It hurts all the way down to my toes."

Two Christian inmates and I gathered around Clyde. We all laid hands on his head. We prayed for his headache to leave. In an hour Clyde was calm and free of pain! Christ had done it!

WEEK FIFTEEN: FOR HEALING

Day 5 ✷ Jesus Healed All Kinds of Diseases

BIBLE VERSE: Large crowds came to him, bringing with them the lame, the blind, the crippled, the dumb, and many other sick people, whom they placed at Jesus' feet; and he healed them.

— Matthew 15:30

PRAYER: I need your healing, Lord. I need you to come into my life with your healing power!

Lord, I pray for your people in prison who are sick. You know their names. You know their hearts and their needs. I pray for your healing power to be on all prisoners in the world who are sick in heart, in mind, or in body. In your name, Jesus. Amen.

THOUGHT FOR THE DAY: Jesus not only healed people one at a time, but he also healed crowds of sick people. People constantly followed him, wanting him to heal them. We can't even imagine the great power that he had to heal. Crippled, blind, injured—and he healed them all!

Jesus can do that today. He could walk into a hospital and heal every patient there! Don't you want to know the Jesus who can do that? You *can* know him!

WEEK FIFTEEN: FOR HEALING

Day 6 ✷ Jesus Can Heal People I Pray For

BIBLE VERSE: Then Jesus said to the officer, "Go home, and what you believe will be done for you." And the officer's servant was healed that very moment.

— Matthew 8:13

PRAYER: I pray now, Lord, for ____________________, who is sick. [Name the person you are praying for who is ill.] I am not there with him [her]. But you are there, as you were with the servant of the soldier. Lord, be with ____________________ and bring healing to him [her].

I also pray for other sick people who have no one else to pray for them, Lord. Bring your healing power to them. In your name. Amen.

THOUGHT FOR THE DAY: Does it do any good to pray for healing for other people? Jesus said it does. The Roman officer came to Jesus asking for healing for his dying servant. Jesus healed the servant even though he wasn't with the servant in person.

Can you pray for someone else in the name of Jesus? *Yes, you can.* Can Jesus hear and answer the prayer? *Yes, he can.* God is not limited in time and space as we are. God can do all things!

WEEK FIFTEEN: FOR HEALING

Day 7 ✷ Jesus Heals Today through Believers

BIBLE VERSE: I am telling you the truth: those who believe in me will do what I do—yes, they will do even greater things, because I am going to the Father.

—John 14:12

PRAYER: I believe in you, Lord Christ. I know you are the Son of God! I truly believe in you! I pray that you will bring healing to God's children in prison who are sick.

I pray too, Lord, for spiritual healing. I pray for those who have trouble doing right. I pray for those who are sick in body and mind. Bring wholeness and healing to God's children in prison, Lord. In your name I pray. Amen.

THOUGHT FOR THE DAY: Faith does not heal, but God can heal through the faith of believers. Do you truly believe in Christ? Christ can heal through your faith.

Ronnie had a high fever. He also had a strained neck and could not turn his head. He was in our camp. We asked Ronnie, "Do you believe in Christ?" "Yes," he said. We laid hands on his head and prayed for healing. His fever was gone the next day, and his neck was straight! Christ heals today!

WEEK SIXTEEN: FOR STRENGTH FROM GOD

Day 1 ✷ To Carry Out Intentions

BIBLE VERSE: "Simon, Simon! Listen! Satan has received permission to test all of you, to separate the good from the bad, as a farmer separates the wheat from the chaff. But I have prayed for you, Simon, that your faith will not fail. And when you turn back to me, you must strengthen your brothers." Peter answered, "Lord, I am ready to go to prison with you and to die with you!"

— Luke 22:31-33

PRAYER: Lord Christ, I have made up my mind to serve you. I have given up sin and evil ways. I am trying to follow you.

But Lord, *I need your strength*! I cannot do this by myself. I keep slipping in my efforts to follow God's will. Pray for me, Lord, as you did for Simon Peter. I want to remain true to you. In your name. Amen.

THOUGHT FOR THE DAY: Jesus warned Simon Peter that Satan desired him. Jesus told Simon that he had prayed for him so that Satan could not have him.

In prison, it is easy to give in to sin and evil. Even when you make up your mind to live for God, there will be times you'll be tempted to return to old ways. Pray. Ask Christ to give you the strength to be faithful to God.

Week Sixteen: For Strength from God

Day 2 ✷ To Hope

Bible Verse: Return, you exiles who now have hope;
return to your place of safety.
Now I tell you that I will repay you
twice over
with blessing for all you have
suffered.
— Zechariah 9:12

Prayer: Time is crawling, God. It seems never to pass. I turn to you for my hope and my strength. They come from nowhere else, Lord, but you. You are the source of all hope. The hope you give me for tomorrow gives me strength to live and to go a day at a time in here. Thank you, Lord. In the name of Jesus. Amen.

Thought for the Day: Prison life drains your strength. You get little sleep and little nutrition from the food. Your emotions and your body are drained. In prison, you need the strength God can give you. Hope in the Lord gives you strength.

Sammy loves the Lord. One day he got a letter telling him he was being charged with another offense in another state. This charge could have added eight years to his sentence. We prayed together and God brought him new hope. Since that time, those new charges were dropped. Place your hope in the Lord. God will give you strength!

WEEK SIXTEEN: FOR STRENGTH FROM GOD

Day 3 ✷ To Practice Faith

BIBLE VERSE: Don't be afraid of anything you are about to suffer. Listen! The Devil will put you to the test by having some of you thrown into prison, and your troubles will last ten days. Be faithful to me, even if it means death, and I will give you life as your prize of victory.

— Revelation 2:10

PRAYER: O God, I'll be honest with you. I'm afraid. I'm scared to death. I'm afraid I will get sick in this awful place. I'm even afraid that I will die here.

But God, in the name of Jesus, I refuse to let this place destroy me. I cast out fear and bring in faith. I am no longer afraid of what might happen to me. I trust in you, Lord. I have faith in you, my God. In the name of Jesus, my Savior. Amen.

THOUGHT FOR THE DAY: A prison is hell on earth. It is a dwelling place for evil. You *must* practice faith in prison. You *must* be a man or woman of God in the midst of this earthly hell. How? Listen to the word of God. "Be faithful to me, even if it means death, and I will give you life as your prize of victory."

In prison, practice and keep your faith for victory in Christ.

WEEK SIXTEEN: FOR STRENGTH FROM GOD

Day 4 ✷ To Trust God

BIBLE VERSE: But I, the LORD, will protect you, and you will not be handed over to the people you are afraid of. I will keep you safe, and you will not be put to death. You will escape with your life because you have put your trust in me. I, the LORD, have spoken.

— Jeremiah 39:17-18

PRAYER: I find it hard to trust, Lord. On my own, I cannot do it. I need your strength within me in order to trust you fully. I pray now for your strength to come into my life so that I will be able to trust in you.

As you delivered Jeremiah from prison, Lord, you can deliver me from this place. I shall not be given into the hands of people who will harm me, O Lord. For you will deliver me! I place my trust in you and you alone. Praise your name! Amen.

THOUGHT FOR THE DAY: Jeremiah was a true man of God. He was a preacher. He was thrown into prison and put in a cell that was underground. But the Lord spoke to him. Through walls, through locked doors, through darkness came the word of the Lord to Jeremiah!

Through the walls and the locked doors comes the word of God to you, friend of the Lord. Praise God!

WEEK SIXTEEN: FOR STRENGTH FROM GOD

Day 5 ✷ To Be Patient

BIBLE VERSE: You need to be patient, in order to do the will of God and receive what he promises.

— Hebrews 10:36

PRAYER: I am trying to do your will, Lord. I am really trying to follow you in my life. Yet it seems that nothing good has happened. It is so hard to wait.

Lord, teach me that doing your will is good in itself. Teach me that I do not have to wait for good things to happen. And Lord, give me strength and patience that I may learn how to wait on you. In the name of Jesus. Amen.

THOUGHT FOR THE DAY: We want things *now.* Sometimes we think if we do the will of God, God will reward us right then. It doesn't always happen that way! Many times it takes longer than we desire.

This means we need *patience.* Patience is the strength of God that enables us to wait without going to pieces. We must not lose faith or hope when we do God's will just because we are not rewarded at once.

You have need of patience. God will give you patience if you ask for it.

WEEK SIXTEEN: FOR STRENGTH FROM GOD

Day 6 ✷ To Wait for God

BIBLE VERSE: Trust in the LORD.
Have faith, do not despair.
Trust in the LORD.
— Psalm 27:14

PRAYER: Waiting is not easy, Lord. The minutes creep by—and then are gone forever. Time I could have spent with my family is wasted in this place. I pray now, Lord, for your strength to enable me to wait on you.

Make me brave so I may pass the hours and the days with you in my heart. Teach me to wait on you, Lord. You have a timetable that is different from mine. Give me your strength as I wait on you and live by your timetable. In Jesus' name I pray. Amen.

THOUGHT FOR THE DAY: James was waiting for word from the parole board. He had been locked up for seven years. He wanted and needed to be with his family and to go to work. The letter came. I saw him sitting on his bed quietly weeping. I knew the news was bad. "Set off a year," he said. Another year! Another useless year of waiting, of sitting in prison while his children grew up without a father and his wife waited for him. "We must learn again *how* to wait," I said. Then we prayed together.

Wait for the LORD;
be strong and let your heart take courage;
wait for the LORD.
—Psalm 27:14, NRSV

WEEK SIXTEEN: FOR STRENGTH FROM GOD

Day 7 ✷ To Endure

BIBLE VERSE: King Zedekiah ordered me to be locked up in the palace courtyard. I stayed there, and each day I was given a loaf of bread from the bakeries until all the bread in the city was gone.

— Jeremiah 37:21

PRAYER: I shall not be destroyed by this prison. God, I was created in your image. I was made for you. In the name of Jesus, I shall endure. I shall last. God, you are giving me the strength to survive. Your power is in my life. Your strength is in my spirit. Thank you, Lord, for your strength and for the power and will to survive. In Jesus' name. Amen.

THOUGHT FOR THE DAY: Jeremiah, the man of God, was cast into prison. He got one piece of bread each day for his meal. When I went to prison, I ate only one meal a day for several weeks. That is all I wanted of that food!

Jeremiah remained. He endured until God delivered him. You need to *endure.* Picture yourself as a rock in the ocean. The waves break over you trying to drown you, trying to wash you out to sea. But you remain there. The waves crash and spill over you—but there you are. *Remain! Endure!* Last in the strength of the Lord.

WEEK SEVENTEEN: TO PRAISE GOD

Day 1 ✹ At All Times

BIBLE VERSE: I will always thank the LORD;
I will never stop praising him.
— Psalm 34:1

PRAYER: O Lord, praise your name! Praise you, Lord! Make me to praise you at all times. When I feel down, when I feel sad, lift my voice in praise, Lord.

I rejoice in praising you all the time. Praises to your name come from my mouth. I praise Jesus, our blessed Redeemer! Sing, O Earth, and proclaim God's wonderful love! Amen.

THOUGHT FOR THE DAY: Praising God can change your life. A guard came to me and asked, "Would you do me a favor? " I said, "I will try. " He said, "Felix here is very sad. He talked about taking his life. Now he doesn't say anything. Would you see what you can do? " I asked Felix to go walking with me. Then I asked him to teach me a song. "There'll be preaching tonight on the old campground," he sang. Then we started running and praising God. Felix said, "I feel better." We did that every evening for a week. Felix began to smile often. His depression lifted when he practiced praising God!

WEEK SEVENTEEN: TO PRAISE GOD

Day 2 ✵ Every Day

BIBLE VERSE: May prayers be said for him at
all times;
may God's blessings be on him
always!

— Psalm 72:15

PRAYER: Praise you, Lord! Praise your name! Holy is the name of Jesus! Holy is the name of Jesus! Holy is your name!

> Thank you, Lord, for saving my soul!
> Thank you, Lord, for making me whole!
> Thank you, Lord, for giving to me!
> Thy great salvation, so rich and free![3]

THOUGHT FOR THE DAY: The first words I speak in the morning are words of praise to God. Words like, *Praise you, Lord!* or *Thank you, Jesus.* And often through the day I speak them again. When I walk or jog in the afternoon, I praise God. I sing, "Praise God from whom all blessings flow."

I praise God in my prayers. Strength and peace come to me each day as I praise God.

---

[3] Permission to reprint words from "Thank You, Lord" by Bessie and Seth Sykes. Copyright 1940 Singspiration Music/ASCAP (chorus). Copyright 1945 Singspiration Music/ASCAP (verses).

WEEK SEVENTEEN: TO PRAISE GOD

Day 3 ✷ When Things Go Well

BIBLE VERSE: Let us, then, always offer praise to God as our sacrifice through Jesus, which is the offering presented by lips that confess him as Lord. Do not forget to do good and to help one another, because these are the sacrifices that please God.

— Hebrews 13:15-16

PRAYER: Praise to you, O God, forever and ever! Thanks be to your name. I will praise you, O God, for all the good things of my life. I thank you for the blessings I have received and that I shall receive.

You are hearing and answering my prayers now, O Lord, and I thank you for that. I thank you for the food you provide for me. I thank you that you are working now to provide my release. Praise you, O God! Amen.

THOUGHT FOR THE DAY: The day I was moved out of the penitentiary was one of the happiest days of my life. The first thing I said was, "Thank you, Jesus!" For it was Jesus who had brought me out, by working through other people. Tears of joy came to my eyes. All I could say was, "Thank you, Lord! Thank you, Lord! Praise God!"

When good things happen to you—whatever they are—*thank God and praise God!*

WEEK SEVENTEEN: TO PRAISE GOD

Day 4 ✷ When Things Go Wrong

BIBLE VERSE: May you always be joyful in your union with the Lord. I say it again: rejoice!

— Philippians 4:4

PRAYER: O Lord, *always* means "always"—even when things go wrong! When things are at their very worst, we are to praise you. Lord, I want to praise you when things are bad for me. But that is so very hard to do. Remind me, O God, in your spirit, to praise you when things go wrong and when things go well.

Praise your name, Lord! I rejoice in you! In the name of Jesus I pray. Amen.

THOUGHT FOR THE DAY: The day I was sentenced was the darkest day in my life. Going to jail! I was separated from my family. I felt embarrassed, humiliated, disappointed. I had expected, hoped, and prayed for a suspended and probated sentence. But I was going to *jail*.

This was the hardest day in my life to praise God. I sat in a tiny crowded cell. I was told I had to sleep on the concrete floor. But I sat down on a bench and said, "Praise the Lord. Thank you, Jesus."

Paul and Silas sang praises to God at midnight in a jail. Praise God when things are at their worst! God will give you strength to cope with whatever situation you are in.

WEEK SEVENTEEN: TO PRAISE GOD

Day 5 ✷ For Family

BIBLE VERSE: They will be as numerous as the specks of dust on the earth. They will extend their territory in all directions, and through you and your descendants I will bless all the nations.

— Genesis 28:14

PRAYER: Our Creator, you are my heavenly Parent! You love me and care for me. But, praise God, others love me too. I thank you, God, for my family. Thank you for [name your family—wife, husband, children, parents, uncle, and others].

I thank you, God, for people who love me and whom I love. No matter what I have done, they still love me. This love they have for me comes from you, Lord. In Jesus' name. Amen.

THOUGHT FOR THE DAY: Billy was coming up for parole. He grew more excited as the date neared. Finally the day came. He met with the parole board. When he came into the barracks, I asked, "How did it go, Billy? " With tears of joy coming down his cheeks, he said, "My mother drove up here 300 miles to be with me." We thanked God for the love his mother had for him.

Somebody in this world loves you. Whoever it is, stop and thank God for the love that person has for you. It is truly a strength in your life!

WEEK SEVENTEEN: TO PRAISE GOD

Day 6 ✷ For Friends

BIBLE VERSE: Then, after Job had prayed for his three friends, the LORD made him prosperous again and gave him twice as much as he had had before.

— Job 42:10

PRAYER: O Lord, thank you for my friends. They love me when they don't have to. They help me and expect nothing in return. They stand by me when others run from me. They come into my life when everyone else goes out.

O Lord, thank you for my friends. And God, teach me to be a friend to someone who needs me. In the name of Jesus. Amen.

THOUGHT FOR THE DAY: I have heard a winning definition of a friend, "A friend is one who comes in when the whole world goes out." When you went to jail, your true friends came forward. The others fell by the wayside.

You have friends. Jesus is one of your friends. "What a Friend we have in Jesus, All our sins and griefs to bear!" (Joseph M. Scriven, 1820–1886) Jesus Christ is your friend! You have others too. Thank God for your friends.

WEEK SEVENTEEN: TO PRAISE GOD

Day 7 ✸ For Life!

BIBLE VERSE: Then the LORD God took some soil from the ground and formed a man out of it; he breathed life-giving breath into his nostrils and the man began to live.

— Genesis 2:7

PRAYER: I praise you, God, for *life*! You gave me life. I am a living soul. I praise you, Lord, that my soul is not in prison—only my body. I thank you that my soul is alive and will live forever.

O God, I confess that at times I have wished I were dead. But I know you love me and that my life still has a purpose for you. I thank you, Lord, for the gift of life and the promise that my life still has in you. Amen.

THOUGHT FOR THE DAY: You have the best gift of all—*life*. God gave you life! You not only have life, but you are *a living soul*.

Your soul cannot be put in prison. No bars, doors, or locks can confine your soul. It is free in Jesus Christ. Let us learn to praise God for the gift of life. Let us know that there is life ahead of us, and if we spend it with Jesus Christ, it will truly be a great life.

WEEK EIGHTEEN: FOR OTHERS (I)

Day 1 ✷ Wife

BIBLE VERSE: Husbands, love your wives just as Christ loved the church and gave his life for it.

— Ephesians 5:25

PRAYER: O God, the most beautiful and precious gift I have ever received is my wife. Thank you for her! Lord, I ask that you watch over her while we are absent from one another. Protect her from harm. Save her from loneliness. Fill her life with hope, peace, and love.

Save her from angry creditors. Help her make it financially, Lord, through this time that I am unable to provide for her needs. Give her peace of mind as she cares for the children, and give her hope for our future. Keep her in good health. In the name of Jesus. Amen.

THOUGHT FOR THE DAY: God *does* watch over our loved ones while we are absent from them. We must ask God to do this. God has watched over my precious wife while this separation has been imposed on us. God has given her strength and the ability to do things and to cope with the world. God has given her friends to help her and persons to pray for her. God has truly watched over her for me.

WEEK EIGHTEEN: FOR OTHERS (I)

Day 2 ✷ Husband

BIBLE VERSE: The LORD will protect you from all
danger;
he will keep you safe.
He will protect you as you come and go
now and forever.
— Psalm 121:7-8

PRAYER: I love my husband, Lord. I ask you now to be with him and protect him from harm while I am in prison. I pray for his continued love for me. I pray that he will stay by me and be true to me while I am here.

Comfort him in my absence, Lord, with your love and peace. When his heart aches, touch it with your healing power. When he is lonely, fill him with your spirit. Bind us ever closer to you and to each other. In Jesus' name. Amen.

THOUGHT FOR THE DAY: Women are in prison too. The world often forgets that. Many women prisoners are married.

If you are a married female prisoner, you are concerned about your husband and your marriage. You need the Lord to watch over him. You need the Lord to save him from loneliness and despair and to keep him ever close to you and to the Lord. The Lord will help you pray for that.

WEEK EIGHTEEN: FOR OTHERS (I)

Day 3 ✱ Preserve Our Marriage

BIBLE VERSE: For this reason a man will leave his father and mother and unite with his wife, and the two will become one.

— Ephesians 5:31

PRAYER: We need you, Lord, to help keep our marriage together. We need you, Lord, to fill our lives with love and hope for the future. We need you to let us know that all things are possible through your power.

God, our marriage was bound in heaven. You joined us together. This forced separation is threatening to undo your work. Cement our marriage anew in your word and will. In Jesus' name. Amen.

THOUGHT FOR THE DAY: The Bible says we shall be joined together in one flesh. But prison creates a pile of broken marriages. We must find it within ourselves to save our homes, and ask God to help us.

Larry's home was breaking up. I prayed for him and even prayed with his wife over the phone. Night after night I prayed for them and their marriage.

You need the power and strength of God to preserve your marriage. Your wife or husband needs that also. God can help hold your marriage together even through the assault of prison life.

WEEK EIGHTEEN: FOR OTHERS (I)

Day 4 ✷ Sweetheart

BIBLE VERSE: May the LORD bless you and take care of you;
May the LORD be kind and gracious to you;
May the LORD look on you with favor and give you peace.
— Numbers 6:24-26

PRAYER: Lord, you know how much I love _________ [name your sweetheart]. You know my heart aches and yearns for her [him]. You know how much, Lord, I desire to be with her [him].

I pray, Lord, that you bless and keep _________ until I can be released and we can get married and have a home. Save our love, Lord, and keep us close together even while I'm here. In Jesus' name. Amen.

THOUGHT FOR THE DAY: As prison destroys marriages, it also destroys courtships and romances. "Out of sight, out of mind" is often a true saying. In addition, the loss of prestige and respect that comes from being in prison can cut the ties of a relationship.

True love comes from God in heaven. It is not made by humankind. And if your love is true, God will bless and keep it for you if you ask God in faith. God can and does bless our sweethearts.

WEEK EIGHTEEN: FOR OTHERS (I)

Day 5 ✷ Children

BIBLE VERSE: I have chosen him in order that he may command his sons and his descendants to obey me and to do what is right and just. If they do, I will do everything for him that I have promised.

— Genesis 18:19

PRAYER: I love my children, Lord. You have given them to me. You love them too. It is hard to support them or take care of them while I am locked up. My children and I need your help, Lord. In the name of Jesus I ask that you help take care of them. I ask that you protect them from harm and sickness. I lift them up to you by name: [name them]. In Jesus' name. Amen.

THOUGHT FOR THE DAY: Are you blessed with children? If you are, be thankful to God. Your children can and will be a blessing to you. It is impossible to support them financially or take care of them while you are locked up. But God will help you. God can do all things!

And you can do something for your children too. You can pray for them. You can ask God to bless and keep them for you. Pray for your children. You are their parent, and they need your love and prayers.

WEEK EIGHTEEN: FOR OTHERS (I)

Day 6 ✷ Mother

BIBLE VERSE: Her children show their appreciation, and her husband praises her.

— Proverbs 31:28

PRAYER: Lord Jesus, you loved your mother. When you were on the cross, you provided for her. I love my mother too, Lord. In your name I call her blessed. She has blessed my life. I thank you for my mother.

But Lord, it is hard to provide for her. I pray to you to help her. Protect her from harm. Save her from loneliness. Mend her broken heart. Bless her and keep her. In your name I pray. Amen.

THOUGHT FOR THE DAY: Is there any greater love in the world, any love purer or stronger than a mother's love? Through the power of God, our Creator, she gave you life. Although she may not always show it, your mother will always love you. In her own way, she is praying for you. Pray for her too. She needs to know that you love her, even though you are locked up.

WEEK EIGHTEEN: FOR OTHERS (I)

Day 7 ✷ Father

BIBLE VERSE: Respect your father and your mother, so that you may live a long time in the land that I am giving you.

— Exodus 20:12

PRAYER: Our Heavenly Father God, I thank you for my earthly father. Thank you that he gave me help and strength. Bless my father, Lord. Keep him from harm and give him your peace. Guide him in all things. Help him be well and strong as he grows older. Comfort him in his thoughts about me. Fill his life with your love and joy. In the name of Jesus. Amen.

THOUGHT FOR THE DAY: When Jesus taught us to pray, he said, "Our Father." We can know God as Father.

We are to respect our fathers as God intended. This is a commandment from God. Your father may not be perfect. He probably is far from perfect. But he is your father. Respect him and pray for him.

If your father is dead, or "gone out of sight," think of God as Father to you. Respect and love your Father.

WEEK NINETEEN: FOR OTHERS (II)

Day 1 ✷ Brothers and Sisters

BIBLE VERSE: Jacob went ahead of them and bowed down to the ground seven times as he approached his brother. But Esau ran to meet him, threw his arms around him, and kissed him. They were both crying.

— Genesis 33:3-4

PRAYER: Lord God, I thank you for my brothers _______________ and for my sisters _______________ [name them]. They are hurting because I am here, Lord. Hold them up with your everlasting arms. Lord, fill them with your spirit. If one of them does not know Jesus Christ as Lord and Savior, I pray for him [her]. In the name of Jesus, bless my brothers and sisters, Lord. Amen.

THOUGHT FOR THE DAY: We often fight with our brothers or sisters. But our brothers and sisters are of our same blood. Jacob and Esau were brothers. They had fought bitterly and then had not seen one another for years.

You need your brothers or sisters to love and support you and to help you in this struggle you are in. You need them, and they need you too. They need to know you will make it and will be there for them in the future.

Give thanks to God if you have a brother or sister. Try to heal any broken places in your relationship with them.

WEEK NINETEEN: FOR OTHERS (II)

Day 2 ✷ Grandmothers and Grandfathers

BIBLE VERSE: I remember the sincere faith you have, the kind of faith that your grandmother Lois and your mother Eunice also had. I am sure that you have it also.

—2 Timothy 1:5

PRAYER: I thank you, Lord, for my grandparents. I remember their faith in you and their love of Jesus. I pray that I may have the faith of my grandmother and of my grandfather while I am in prison.

Lord, I ask you to love and protect my grandparents in these, their later years. May your loving arms surround them and keep them near to you. In Jesus' name. Amen.

THOUGHT FOR THE DAY: The love of a grandmother or grandfather is very special. Many people today are raised by a grandparent while their mother and father work or if there is only one parent in the home. If your grandmother(s) or grandfather(s) are living, you know that they love you and you love them.

Thank you, Lord, for grandparents in our time of need!

WEEK NINETEEN: FOR OTHERS (II)

Day 3 ✷ Other Christians

BIBLE VERSE: Do all this in prayer, asking for God's help. Pray on every occasion, as the Spirit leads. For this reason keep alert and never give up; pray always for all God's people.

— Ephesians 6:18

PRAYER: God, you created *all* people—black, brown, red, white, yellow. You don't recognize color or race, God. I pray for *all* people everywhere in the world—in Africa, Asia, South America, our own continent and our own country, and everywhere else as well.

God, I also pray for your children who are in prison. Bless them, hold them up, and give them strength. Help them to believe in themselves. Help them to keep their faith in you. In Jesus' name I pray. Amen.

THOUGHT FOR THE DAY: I was talking with Larry. Larry is becoming a Christian. "There are millions of Christians over the world," I said. "Surely Jesus is real. He is real in my life too."

Christians all over the world need to be prayed for. They need the people of God in prison to pray for them that they will do God's work and be God's people. Pray for Christians all over the world. They need your prayers.

WEEK NINETEEN: FOR OTHERS (II,

Day 4 ✷ Fellow Inmates

BIBLE VERSE: So then, confess your sins to one another and pray for one another, so that you will be healed. The prayer of a good person has a powerful effect.

—James 5:16

PRAYER: God, today I pray for ______________ [name fellow inmates]. I lift them up to you. I pray that they may give their lives and hearts to you. Fill them with your Holy Spirit. Bless them, Lord. If they are having problems, help them to find the right answers.

I pray for their families, Lord. I pray for their release. I pray for their health and for their souls. In the name of Jesus, I pray for my fellow inmates. Amen.

THOUGHT FOR THE DAY: I thank God for friends I have made in prison. You may wonder if I'm serious. Yes, I am. I have made friends here who will be friends the rest of my life. They are friends who love the Lord.

People of God in prison have prayed for me. I have a prayer pact with one. Your fellow inmates need you to pray for them. You need them to pray for you. God will bless your prayers.

Pray for your fellow inmates. They need your prayers! Ask your fellow inmates to pray for you. You need their prayers!

EEN: FOR OTHERS (II)

er Prisoners in the World

BIBL… …ORD looked down from his
holy place on high,
he looked down from heaven to earth.
He heard the groans of prisoners
and set free those who were
condemned to die.
And so his name will be
proclaimed in Zion,
and he will be praised in Jerusalem.
— Psalm 102:19-21

PRAYER: I pray to you, my God. You are everybody's God. I pray for all prisoners in the world. In every country on earth where men and women, boys and girls, are kept in prison—I pray for them. Many are tired. Many are confused. Many are sick. Many are hungry. All of them are your children. All are persons for whom your Son Jesus Christ died on the cross. God, fill them now with your love. Let them know Jesus died for their salvation. In the name of Jesus. Amen.

THOUGHT FOR THE DAY: God knows the prisoners of the world. In every country where people are locked up, God knows each of them. Many have been beaten, robbed, and starved. Prisoners in the world are suffering people. Let all of us pray for them. Jesus died for them too!

Week Nineteen: For Others (II)

Day 6 ✳ Enemies

Bible Verse: Bless those who curse you, and pray for those who mistreat you.

— Luke 6:28

Prayer: It hurts to be cursed, Lord Jesus. You know that. You were cursed when you carried the cross down the street of Jerusalem. You were cursed as you went to the cross. Yet you did not curse anyone in return. You prayed for those who hurt and cursed you.

And you came out victorious! Lord, give me strength to bless those who curse me. Give me the grace of God to pray for those who hurt me or try to destroy me. I pray in your name. Amen.

Thought for the Day: Maya Angelou wrote, "The New Testament informs the reader that it is more blessed to give than to receive. I have found that among its other benefits, giving liberates the soul of the giver."[4]

This is doubly true of forgiveness. As we forgive those who curse us, we are the ones who benefit the most. Our souls are truly made free.

When we pray for those who have mistreated us, they are blessed and helped. But we are blessed and helped even more than they! When we pray for our enemies, we are the ones most blessed!

---

[4]Maya Angelou, *Wouldn't Take Nothing for My Journey Now* (New York: Random House, 1993), p. 15.

WEEK NINETEEN: FOR OTHERS (II)

Day 7 ✷ For the Spirit to Intercede

BIBLE VERSE: The Spirit also comes to help us, weak as we are. For we do not know how we ought to pray; the Spirit himself pleads with God for us in groans that words cannot express.

— Romans 8:26

PRAYER: O God, I don't know what to pray for. But you know. I ask the Holy Spirit to pray for me and to pray for people I don't know but who need prayer. I ask the Holy Spirit to pray for goals I don't know about for my life. But above all, I ask the Holy Spirit to pray for your will to be done for your people. In Jesus' name. Amen.

THOUGHT FOR THE DAY: "Amazing grace! How sweet the sound!" God loves you so much that God even makes prayers *for you* through the Holy Spirit. Imagine that! You don't know *whom* to pray for? God knows. And the Holy Spirit prays for you even when you don't know what to pray for or how to pray.

How does the Spirit pray for you? Just ask God that question and the Spirit will pray for you!